SELECTED P

RICHARD CRASHAW was born in Lond
theologian and preacher. He was e
London, then Pembroke College Car
Peterhouse in 1635, from which he w
to conform to Puritan demands. He went into exile on the continent
and converted to Rome around 1645, dying (possibly poisoned, more
likely of consumption) in Loreto in 1649.

ROBIN HOLLOWAY is a composer, though read English at Cambridge
in the early 1960s. He is a Life Fellow of Caius College, and retired
from a personal chair in musical composition at the University in
2011.

FyfieldBooks aim to make available some of the great classics of British and European literature in clear, affordable formats, and to restore often neglected writers to their place in literary tradition.

FyfieldBooks take their name from the Fyfield elm in Matthew Arnold's 'Scholar Gypsy' and 'Thyrsis'. The tree stood not far from the village where the series was originally devised in 1971.

> *Roam on! The light we sought is shining still.*
> *Dost thou ask proof? Our tree yet crowns the hill,*
> *Our Scholar travels yet the loved hill-side*

from 'Thyrsis'

RICHARD CRASHAW

Selected Poems
Secular & Sacred

Chosen and Introduced by
ROBIN HOLLOWAY

FyfieldBooks

CARCANET

First published in Great Britain in 2013 by
Carcanet Press Limited
Alliance House
Cross Street
Manchester M2 7AQ

www.carcanet.co.uk

A CIP catalogue record for this book is available from the British Library

ISBN 978 1 84777 233 6

The publisher acknowledges financial assistance from Arts Council England

Typeset by XL Publishing Services, Exmouth
Printed and bound in England by SRP Ltd, Exeter

Contents

Intermezzo II

III   Sacred, Part 2: *Carmen Deo Nostro*

Acknowledgements

My initial debt is to Michael Schmidt of Carcanet, who so readily acceded to the suggestion that I would love to undertake this book and so promptly followed it up with the practicalities. Some 48 years before, my copy of L.C. Martin's Oxford English Texts edition of Crashaw had been a gift from John Casey of King's College, Cambridge, then Caius: a tome much-treasured and perused ever since.

Thereafter, current friends and colleagues have provided both encouragement and counsel: among them John Kerrigan of St John's, Cambridge; Colin Burrow of All Souls, Oxford; Sarah Howe and Sarah Houghton-Walker of my own Cambridge college; and Sophie Read of Christ's, Cambridge, who kindly allowed advance access to the chapter on Crashaw in her forthcoming book.

The principal debt is to Alex Wong of the poet's own Cambridge college, Peterhouse; generous with his time, his knowledge, his talents, not only providing when requested his own choice for this Latinless reader of the Latin epigrams, but adding, unsolicited, his elegant English versions, then throwing in, also unasked, the complete new 160-line *Bulla* for good measure!

I'm beholden to all these: and have been pleased and touched to find such easy exchange of scholarly and critical information across departments, institutions and individuals, sometimes opaque to each other. Neither scholar nor critic myself, I've benefitted the more from their assistance in making my own decisions and expressing my own views with untrammelled freedom.

L.C. Martin's aforementioned excellent edition of the complete works in all Crashaw's three languages for the Oxford English Texts first appeared in 1927: its second edition (1957) is the basis for the poems selected and reprinted here, as its biographical introduction and textual material for my few facts. I am grateful to Oxford University Press for permission to use Martin's edition as my source-text. George Walton Williams re-edited the works in 1972 (New York University Press); and a new edition is forthcoming from Richard Rambuss of Brown University. Martin and Williams are difficult to find, while the new complete edition will undoubtedly be way beyond students' pockets: I therefore believe that the present slim quintessence fulfils an important role in providing an accessible introduction to the work of this great English poet.

Robin Holloway
Gonville and Caius College, Cambridge, July 2012

Introduction

Mention Crashaw to the poetry-lover and one is virtually certain to be answered with 'portable and compendious oceans' – if Crashaw has been heard of at all. In that classic anthology of bad verse *The Stuffed Owl* (1930) Crashaw doesn't figure in the main selections, but one line only (one of his finest, properly taken) flavours the preliminary *hors d'oeuvres*. Dwight MacDonald's excellent book of *Parodies* for Faber (1961) prints the 'oceans' stanza complete, the first in fourteen instances of 'self-parody (unconscious)'. Crashaw also appears in the *Penguin Anthology of Sick Verse*, and no doubt elsewhere. To see him as inherently absurd has become a reflex action, a received opinion.

There is no question that this poet *does* give hostages to fortune, raising barriers of taste in subject matter and, especially, treatment of it, that are hard to pass. In all that epoch of Metaphysical extravagances he is most extravagant of all; but not with the play of a Marvell or the fun of a Cleveland. On the contrary, he evinces fervour too easily dismissed as perfervid, and religious intensity as fanaticism – qualities, or perhaps disqualifications, that a would-be advocate must endeavour to avoid! Since student days I have loved the best of him, and passing years have confirmed my view that he is among the greatest English poets – 'for some things'. Plainly the range is not wide: other things, maybe most things, are outside it. But once within, the marksmanship is spot on, on a target attempted by few of his peers at the time or since. *My* aim is simpler. I hope, by choices negative as well as positive, to vindicate a poet whose achievement, albeit acknowledged narrow and special, is rare in the language and of very high calibre. In doing so I must necessarily confront difficulties, reservations, *déplorations* ('*Richard Crashaw, hélas*'), rebut them if possible, certainly not evade them.

First, though, an outline of his life:

> Born on the turn of 1612/13, son of William Crashaw (1572–1625/6), emphatically Protestant preacher and writer on religious themes, originally from the neighbourhood of Sheffield, holding various Yorkshire benefices, finally one in East London.
>
> 1629 enters Charterhouse; receives thorough grounding in 'the choicest Orators & Poets of Greek and Latin. Already composing in English too.
>
> July 1631 enters Pembroke College, Cambridge, on a scholar-

ship whose duties include writing epigrams in the classical languages upon Biblical subjects, harmoniously compatible with his ardent Laudian Anglicanism.

1635 Fellowship at Peterhouse (main focus of the high church in Cambridge): soon followed by position as catechist, and curacy at the closely associated adjacent church of Little St Mary's. Associated also with the community at Little Gidding. Active as poet, valued as preacher, closely involved with enriching the ornamental iconography both of his college chapel and the church alongside, as also in their musical activities. These Cambridge years viewed from later exile and disappointment as a 'little contentful kingdom'.

Early 1640s, the Peterhouse group's high church/Royalist sympathies come under ever severer threat in Parliamentary eastern counties. 1643, Cambridge occupied by rebel forces. The scenes of his loving attentions vandalised by the Parliamentary Commissioners (at Peterhouse 'We pulled down 2 mighty great Angells with Wings, & divers other Angells ... & about a hundred Chirubims & Angells & divers Superstitious Letters in gold': at Little St Mary's 'We broke down 60 Superstitious Pictures, Some Popes & Crucyfixes & God the father sitting in a chayer & holding a Glasse in his hand'). Probably already self-exiled before the official ejection from his Fellowship in April 1644.

Exile: Holland initially, possibly Liège, certainly Leyden; Paris by 1645. During this troubled period, converted to Roman Catholicism, apparently without seeking the priesthood.

1646 Henrietta Maria intercedes on his behalf for a post in Rome, without success. Great need, and indications of failing health. 1647 a post found in Cardinal Palotto's household at Rome, wherein Crashaw did not fit, complaining of the impiety of the Italians in the Cardinal's retinue. April 1649 moved, perhaps on compassionate grounds, to a humble position serving the shrine of Our Lady at Loreto: travelled there that summer, dying there August 21, only a month or so after arriving, 'of a Feaver, the holy order of his soul over-heating his body'.

Crashaw has been marginalised as well as divisive down the centuries. Problems begin with the earliest editions, fugitive and erratic, none of his own direct making, published at home in distracted times, in exile with little hope of dissemination. Their texts confusingly overlap – he was a born fiddler. The evident turn towards concentration and non-extremity in his third volume is cut off by his early death; but already his conversion, his subject matter and its treatment, had put his work out of the tenor of the English temperament. He possibly would have succeeded better, outstanding in the language, as a poet in Latin, the lingua franca of artistic/intellectual communication, reaching the whole of Counter-Reformation Europe rather than the lost connexion to his native land. Thus from the start he is awkward and oblique: the only place and time he wholly belonged to was the Cambridge circle of the early 1640s centred upon the 'little contentful kingdom' of Peterhouse and Little St Mary's. His friend and fellow-poet Joseph Beaumont in particular shows many parallels of thought, feeling, expression; Beaumont's favoured genre, the poem devoted to a particular saint, reaches its high point in Crashaw's *Hymn to St. Teresa*. Despite striking individual moments Beaumont (whose spiritual epic *Psyche* eventually clocked in at 24 cantos) is a tepid poetaster compared with Crashaw even on an ordinary day – and at his best Crashaw is simply extraordinary.

When the Metaphysical manner went out, the Augustan age had no place for him. Pope, who could and did use Donne as a model, gives a few condescending and not wholly unappreciative opinions concerning his fellow-Catholic in a letter of 1710. But he's not in the *Lives of the Poets*, nor even mentioned in Johnson's well known animadversions over the preceding century's manner in the *Life of Cowley*. The placid plains of later eighteenth-century verse suited him least of all, though we now can discern analogies with its disturbed eccentric outsiders Smart and Blake that would have made all three unacceptable, indeed meaningless, to prevalent taste.

Crashaw was differently alien to the Romantics, though there is Coleridge's enigmatic remark that the lines on St Teresa 'were ever present to my mind whilst writing the second part of Christabel; if, indeed, by some subtle process of the mind they did not suggest the first thought of the whole poem'. And we can now perceive that aspects of Keats tending towards the tacky and sickly – the 'sticky blisses' and 'embarrassments' so tactfully explored by Christopher Ricks – are comparable in sensibility, even in language. Supposedly closer, in fact incompatible, are Shelley's mystic-sensuous ravings; while the visionary element in Wordsworth is as different from Crashaw's as worsted from satin. Nor has the Age of Tennyson any compatibility whatsoever, though Crashaw does figure in an interesting list drawn up by John Clare when planning an anthology of early British poets. Browning rhymes rather with Donne for twisty complexity and arcane learning worn lightly or heavily. With

Hopkins there are circumstantial parallels – the conversion, the fervour and intensity, the extreme nature of the imagery and diction, the early death burnt out by the spirit within: and at the end of the century Francis Thompson is warmly appreciative.

With the early twentieth century comes a change in the light which, nonetheless, doesn't shine very brightly for Crashaw. He's absolutely out for Pound, of course. Eliot provided a *Note* in *For Lancelot Andrewes* (1928) whose principal ploy is to compare Crashaw's imagery with Shelley's to the earlier poet's advantage. But Eliot's outstanding Metaphysical is Donne, with Marvell in the wings. Thence *Revaluation* and *Seven Types*. Crashaw is missing from the former, present in the latter for glances askance, foil for better ambiguities elsewhere – a line continued much later by Ricks. A seminal essay of 1925 by Mario Praz appears to originate the view that Crashaw is most justly appreciated as an artist of the high continental Counter-Reformation, comparable with Bernini: an insight developed at book length by Austin Warren in *Richard Crashaw: A Study in Baroque Sensibility*. Another pioneering effort was Ruth Wallerstein's *Richard Crashaw: A Study in Style and Poetic Development* (1935).

The post-war period has seen intermittent attention in several monographs and symposia; more frequent, in general studies of the half-century or so of English Metaphysical poetry wherein Crashaw is a sort of 'absent presence'. A biography by Thomas Healy appeared in the 1980s. I've deliberately not consulted any of this literature, not wanting to be beholden, nor indeed influenced, either in choices or views.

So Crashaw is no longer neglected, but still cannot be called mainstream, and maybe never will be: it's the nature of the case, which I must now proceed to probe.

Taste, sometimes almost viscerally, is the sticking-point. He offends the proprieties equally in religious sentiment as in artistic decorum. The perceived ideal for both in seventeenth-century English devotional poetry (indeed for all subsequent epochs however styles and idioms change) is Herbert – simple, frugal, whose extremes high or low are thoroughly tempered to reach a middle way without blandness, passionate within demureness, unimpugnable in doctrine and expression; in facture spare, precise, exact even to tightness, compacting untold wealth of content by implication.

The nature of Crashaw's art couldn't be more different: its forms burgeon and gush and sprawl, its language is that of unabashed amorous eroticism, its feelings of ultimate perfervour. The omnipresent imagery of kisses/blisses, yielding/succumbing, infusion/penetration (always passive and 'feminine'), evokes masochistic ecstasies that court ridicule, pity, disgust. All this leaves no hope for a middle way of restraint and carefulness: he is usually in a hot flush, even torrid, tumultuous and risk-taking. Yet paradoxes abound: the stance is also at the same time curiously chaste; there's no gasping or yearning, panting or heaving: never cool let alone cold, he can advocate '[n]ought too hot within' without insincerity. Innately sensuous even unto sensuality he yet avoids gross carnality: all is subsumed into a 'hard gemlike flame' by which he is consumed without being devoured: a Burning Bush. There must be a word, eluding this vain attempt to encapsulate, for his characteristic tone and the means whereby it is achieved. *Sublimation* is the most obvious – of sexual into spiritual, physical into metaphysical, thick heavy fleshliness into weightless ethereal purity. But sublimation doesn't quite do it: it's not a substitution as by transaction moral or commercial – it's his manner of comprehending and transmuting mystical experience, via carnal imagery, into artistic form.

Odes and *Hymns* are the forms/genres that best embody this kind of impulse. Mostly they come without articulation by stanza, but are by no means therefore shapeless: a stream, an effusion, a rhapsodic improvisation to be sure; thence shaped by rigorous classical training, strenuous mastery of rhetorical exercises, the disciplines of theological thought, the practice of the liturgy and the delivery of sermons. All such solid stuff underlies the lacy lyric surface, all surge and dance – 'kicking the curled heads of conspiring stars' (to adapt the ravishing line singled out on page 1 of *The Stuffed Owl* for its absurdity), suppling and melting it into airy liquid flow.

Such flexibility of structure, rhythm, line-length, enjambment, tends when not good to drool on as though on autopilot. Even when good – great – supreme, a sense of 'automatic writing' can still remain. At its best, Crashaw's verse combines the apparently opposite advantages of looseness, flow and spontaneity with tautness of localised rhythm and overall structure – no formalist straitjacket, but no mere uncontrolled oil-gush. This compatibility of opposites gives the greatest poems their shape, rather than their argument as such. There's often no solid paraphrasable content beyond the given subject (the Name of Jesus, say) and its associated cluster of words. These words drift or rush by into successions and processions of related ideas in a way scarcely resembling 'what is ordinarily called thinking'. Of its nature this entails much repetition, within individual poems and across from poem to poem over the entire canon – which, seen as a whole, may sometimes recall the actress who runs the gamut of emotions 'from A to B'. He is always the same, limited but not narrow or shallow, just as clouds or waves or leaves, always reforming from the same basic motions, give similar but never identical results. Formulaic, minimalist, pattern-making, so much so as to be sometimes – sometimes at its very best – well-nigh abstract: a stream of consciousness/unconsciousness unchanging yet never stepped into twice; free association taken down in a trance, rapt-out-of-the-world; surreal/transparent/evanescent/nonsensical/lovely as Ashbery!

Yet never, despite all-too-likely opportunities, going slack. *Wit* still informs this poet at the furthest remove from the poetic culture of his times. Born into it willy-nilly, he inherits a grounding in Greek and Latin equally with humanism and Biblical exegesis, the appetite for learning and brainwork that charges the Zeitgeist from Donne to Milton. Chewy and knotty with both of these, at the other end extravagant, gay, playful, ostentatious – Cleveland, Benlowes *et al.*, emblematic and didactic in Quarles, sober and exemplary in Herbert, going soft and silly in Cowley, lying behind the cheerfullest frivolity of Herrick and the Cavaliers out of Ben. Only Marvell is able to get elements of all these diversities into one span – his gamut runs from A to Z.

Crashaw retains the epoch's play of intelligence even when his verse's *content* consists of abstractions dissolved into ecstasies of automatic writing, table-tapping, 'nonsense', as just described. By the end of the seventeenth century its earlier ideal of wit, characterised in Maynard Mack's *Life of Pope* as 'freewheeling acts of imagination … packed into puns, paradoxes, subversive ambiguities, outrageous metaphors, explosive yokings of opposites' has contracted into merely what Dryden called 'a propriety of thoughts and words'. Crashaw emphatically belongs with the earlier *embarras* rather than the succeeding decorum; unique through his intense and specialised focus but demonstrably related to his contemporaries via the air they all breathed.

Meaning, finally: the last hurdle: what does this poetry *mean*, both in itself, and, more pressingly, to readers of nowadays who, however sympathetically inclined and curious for a different voice alongside familiar rewards and admirations, are unlikely to extend much credit to an art born of nothing if not the most ardent and urgent Catholic faith?

Meaning in the most direct sense is not problematic: Crashaw's vocabulary and thought are pellucid, his paradoxes and the shocks and surprises of his imagery never recondite, however (sometimes extremely) ingenious. Any reference to the scriptures is easily check-able: but if the reader is not a latterday Laudian high-churcher à la Eliot or, more crucially, a Roman Catholic *dévote*, the *essential* meaning of Crashaw's religious work, indeed its *raison d'être*, must surely go missing entirely? I myself 'don't believe a word of it', and this is without doubt the majority position, commonplace though it be. To make it full rather than emptied-out, positive rather than abject, is the prime object of the present selection of a totally *engagé* religious artist – an enterprise analogous to 'rescuing' whole centuries of liturgical music for the practising atheist whose disbe-lief is well past help, let alone the vast regions of religious art on canvas, in stone, wood, glass, metal, ivory, where the discrepancies are still more desperate.

Above all I don't want to say that the pleasure taken by the non-faithful 'suspends disbelief' and is simply aesthetic. The cruellest expression of detached *dis*-engagement is Remy de Gourmont's in *The Problem of Style* (1902) – 'he who enjoys the literary beauty of a sermon by Bossuet cannot be touched by it religiously, and he who weeps for the death of Ophelia has no aesthetic sense'. Too drastic! I prefer the amelioration suggested in a recent offhander from Charles Rosen, speaking (apropos a comparable conflict over Romanesque sculptures) of 'a clear aesthetic energy independent of sacred meaning'.[1]

Yet to concede this much might be too tepid and beige.

Let me try to regain a more central ground by physiologising, psychologising, humanising, the experience of reading some of Richard Crashaw's most unapologetic, most flagrantly Catholic utterances – the *Hymn to St Teresa* for instance, or the *Hymn on the Assumption of the Virgin*. What's Teresa to us (though at least she really existed and wrote a celebrated, widely disseminated auto-biography)? What's this Assumption? Who is this improbable/

---

1   And this, halfway: Matisse – 'When I see Giotto's frescoes in Padua, I don't worry about knowing which particular scene of the *Life of Christ* I have before my eyes, but I immediately grasp the feeling that comes from it, for that is in the lines of the composition, in the colour, and the title can only confirm my first impression.'

absurdist Virgin? It all serves but for laughter, pity, scorn. But everyone enjoys sweets, delicious smells, slides and airlifts, swings and roundabouts, dreamboats, the London Eye and the Eiffel Tower, ski-ing, being tossed in a blanket, rolling down a grassy slope, swimming weightless, swirling patterns of music, dreaming of flying, being tickled till we laugh ourselves silly. Let alone more intimate bodily pleasures, adult rather than childish, plural and singular, straight or curvaceous. No one in (literally) their senses will deny the common humanity of all this. Take all such raptures into their not-impossible spiritual dimension. Bodily gratifications of every kind, decidedly including the carnal/amorous/erotic, are related directly upon a sort of Enlightenment calculus to the inner life of the mind and spirit – soul, to use a not-altogether-forgotten idea – irrespective of the outer existence of utilitarian dailiness.

Irrespective too of belief, dogma, practice of a set religion with its thou-shalt-not prohibitions, framed (it can easily seem) to be transgressed, though in fact strangely akin to the utterances of mystics from the dawn of Christianity, the *Song of Songs* setting the tune, right down to St Teresa, her spiritual companion St John of the Cross, and beyond (albeit firmly passing by Calvin, Knox, Savonarola, Wesley, St Cardinal Newman, Mrs Baker Eddy *et al.* on the other side). In this context Crashaw's religious verse opens out from a content dogmatically sectarian into a content of *jouissance* shared by humanity at large.

Equally, everyone is prone to doubt, worry, error, vacillation, dither and delay, resisting the known and needed good, subject to frigidity or dryness, haunted by waste and futility, marked by sullen refusal to break out of the self-perpetuating circle of spiritual frowardness, clutching at wilfully *low* views, *meanness* of outlook, *narrowness* of understanding, *meagre* tolerance, escalating downwards into depression all-too-literally – a long flat dull prospect without hope. Such a poem as *A Letter from Mr Crashaw to the Countess of Denbigh, Against Irresolution and Delay in Matters of Religion* addresses such universals way beyond its declared initial purpose, absolutely irrespective of Christian belief in any of its confusing and pusillanimous sectarian differences let along the particular situation of the said Countess (who she? though she did at least really exist). Anyone and everyone can empathise here, such is the poet's sovereign command of ravishing and irresistible persuasive force. The explicit original aim is changed utterly into a general truth transcending the doctrinaire/ideological as surely as it transcends the merely aesthetical.

If such larger issues are granted in his favour, objections to Crashaw's particular excesses and general tastelessness can be readily dispersed. The endless recyclings of his imagery and its tendency towards sweet sticky sickliness are best seen as conventional; decorative adjuncts, innate to the epoch in its prevalent artistic and religious practices. No one (in their senses) complains about putti, haloes, fluttering doves, 'mighty great Angells with Wings' in many centuries of visual iconography, nor indeed about conventional rhetorical and ornamental formulae, opening and closing clichés, etc. in many centuries of music: why then in words? Everyone delights in scrolls of reiterated pattern-work, acanthus leaves, tops to Corinthian columns, etc. – gaping tritons spewing water in fountains, straining muscle-men and writhing maidens supporting cornices or balconies. We no longer feel the need to call the thought-police to protest that the crime of the ornament has been committed. Similarly, the ostensibly mechanical symmetries and repetitions dominating devotional practice – the sequences, amens, alleluias, Kyrie eleisons and Agnus Dei's (etc.) of the liturgy, gone though over and over again, never changing, always new for its true celebrants and true participants. And this is to focus the scope again upon the religion that was for this great poet his Alpha to Omega, the entire world of experience and understanding, contained within his work, generously interpreted, for all its readers of any persuasion or none.

Choice and Shape of this Selection

This is absolutely a personal selection, relying upon taste, ear, pleasure, feeling, as criteria and guides. Undisputed masterpieces are all present, complete, usually (not always) in their later versions. But there are some total omissions that might raise Crashavian eyebrows. Elsewhere I've not scrupled to make cuts within poems of calibre, or excerpt a few finer passages from a mediocre context.

The plan is at once circular and teleological. First (after the finest lines from Cowley's *Elegy*) comes a small selection from the best of Crashaw's secular verse: *Delights of the Muses* (London, 1646). No disagreement over *Music's Duell*, virtuoso set piece, descant upon a favourite subject, the contest between nature (the bird, always a nightingale) and art; based upon the Latin original of Famianus Strada (enormously expanded by Crashaw); a triumph of hyperbole and eventual, surprising, pathos. *Wishes to his (supposed) Mistresse*, another celebrated piece albeit more divisive, is given in its final version, much expanded from a starting point of only ten triolets (1641). The play of tender dream-fantasy – 'my fictions ... her story' seems to me perfect in delicacy of feeling, felicitous in form as in diction – sensuous appreciation and chaste demureness in lovely equipoise: but it has caused displeasure, even offence. It is preceded here by three miniatures associated in subject – the *Epitaph on a Young Married Couple*, a two-line epigram concerning marriage and the single life, and the clearly related *Author's Motto*. The version of Lessius (in a later revision re-entitled *Temperance, the Cheap Physician*!) has its moments. The *Epithalamium* is included as unique instance in Crashaw's output of a familiar genre: clearly not up to the marvellous examplars in Spenser or Herrick; charged, though, with characteristic imagery and with many parallels in his wholly religious verse, (recalling the stop-press note to the 1646 volume – 'Reader, there was a sudden mistake ('tis too late to recover it) thou wilt quickly find it out, and I hope as soone passe it over, some of the humane Poems are misplaced among the Divine'). The Coronation piece and the poem on a foul morning give just two specimens from the uncollected and here otherwise unrepresented early secular output, arguably best of an undistinguished bunch that includes other royal Occasions, panegyrics to nobility, and three upon the Gunpowder Plot. Most of this, whether ungathered or included in *Delights*, is eminently ditchable.

Now comes the first of two *intermezzi*. It begins with two slight neatly turned compliments to poets overlapping from Crashaw's Cambridge years: to his precocious junior Abraham Cowley (born 1618: his *Poetical Blossoms* 1633) – complementary too, accompanying the gift of two unripe 'apricockes', its lightweight wittiness fore-shadowing decadent 'rococo' Metaphysical still to come, Cowley its principal proponent. The other is a dedication to his famous senior George Herbert (1593–1633: *The Temple* issued first, posthumously, the year of his death) – complementary by anticipation of work still to come; fanciful, sweet unto succulence, *vis-à-vis* sage and sober. Next, a selection from his thirteen elegies for university friends – again a familiar genre wherein he cannot compare with the most celebrated. Two given here complete, plus the prettiest lines from five others, show the poet in touchingly humane mode, often lost on later, higher flights.

Crashaw translated only Book I of Marino's four-book epic *La Strage de gli Innocenti*: its 66 stanze can't be reprinted here in full, and probably wouldn't much reward the general reader if they were. I've selected a few memorable moments (Crashaw is as always freely inventive with his source), and provided their context with the text.

This first *intermezzo* ends with Crashaw's longest Latin poem complete: *Bulla*, the *Bubble*, a *tour de force* of fantasy whose sustained flights of invention have been captured and brought to life in recent times in a major orchestral piece by Elliott Carter, his *Symphonia: sum fluxae pretium spei* of 1993–96 (its three movements all given a different motto from the poem: the overall title, 'I am the prize of inconstant hope', better rendered here as 'I am the reward of tran-sitory hope'). The Bubble, floating free and transparent above the earth's surface, is described in all her phases – now hilarious, fickle, and vague; now taking a darker view, perceiving the folly of mankind under sway of the blind goddess Fortuna; eventually disappearing with an iridescent twang into thin air. Made of nothing (she says, in her own voice), if I bore you I can easily be pricked.

Next comes a first selection of Sacred Poems, the heart of the corpus. The *Preface* to the volume here excerpted, *Steps to the Temple* (London, 1646), is so eloquent, interesting, charming, germane, as to justify its presence uncut. Persuasively attributed to Crashaw's friend and fellow-poet at Peterhouse Joseph Beaumont: but if not his, surely born of affection, rapport, and tender feeling – 'Look on his following leaves, and see him breathe'.

Many of the poems in *Steps* recur in Crashaw's next and last publication *Carmen Deo Nostro* (basis of this selection's closing section); amplified and altered, usually but not invariably to their advantage. My choice of text here and later is not consistent: I've been guided by instinct rather than chronology and editorial exactness, sometimes committing what would be inappropriate to a scholarly publication, a conflation of earlier and later versions. As remarked before, the poet was a born fiddler, now enhancing his original on a revisit, now over-egging and spoiling, now a bit of both.

We now encounter some of the finest, and some of the most notorious, of his work. The latter first: *The Weeper*, which of all gives most licence to detraction and mockery. Here the earlier version is clearly preferable to the revision – 23 rather than 31 stanze, fresher, purer, less overwrought and overfraught. (It also has the advantage of excluding those 'portable and compendious oceans' by which Crashaw is best/worst known, though both texts include the nearly as notorious 'Upwards dost thou weep'.) The subject was popular on the continent, indeed a bit of a cliché. Crashaw begs, borrows and steals from his predecessors, most notably the curious stanza-shape from Marino's sequence on the perennial theme. As always he repays what he takes with his own lavish and curious richness of freedom, even when risking, perhaps knowingly, smiles, or outright laughter. Next, *The Teare*, almost a continuation of *The Weeper* (one early edition uses an identical stanza in both): the same subject, mood, form, in a string of near-self-contained epigrams – beads on a Rosary.

The *Nativity Hymn*, 'sung as by the Shepheards', is an enchanting pastoral cantata: this later version brings out the choral refrains more clearly than the earlier, not so much prompting a musical setting as already containing by implication its own. I've preferred it to its successor, the *Epiphany Hymn* 'sung as by the Three Kings', longer but with somehow less to it, the Shepherds' tribute naive, rustic, songful, offering their lambs 'to thee, dread lamb!'; the Kings' complex, witty, learnéd, tortuous, offering at last (only after some 240 lines, by which time the Shepherds' chorus has long since finished and they've all gone home) their rich and useless gifts, 'to which He now has no pretence'.

The *Hymn in honour of St Teresa* is by common consent the central masterpiece; even Crashaw's detractors acknowledge that here he reaches places touched by no other poet in English. The later text is altogether preferable verbally and in terms of punctuation; but the Hymn is laid out here in its earlier divisions into irregular indented stanze: this helps with articulation and architecture, giving visible breathing spaces, letting air in onto the burning fires that sustain this superb performance from ecstasy to ecstasy. The unbroken flow can become a bit of a strain. Two sources from the Saint's autobiography inspire the poet; first, the episode from her childhood, taken from Book I in an early twentieth-century translation:

> One of my brothers was nearly of my own age; and he it was whom I most loved, though I was very fond of them all, and they of me. He and I used to read Lives of Saints together. When I read of martyrdom undergone by the Saints for the love of God, it struck me that the vision of God was very cheaply purchased; and I had a great desire to die a martyr's death – not out of any love of Him of which I was conscious, but that I might most quickly attain to the fruition of those great joys of which I read that they were reserved in Heaven; and I used to discuss with my brother how we could become martyrs. We settled to go together to the country of the Moors, begging our way for the love of God, that we might be there beheaded; and our Lord, I believe, had given us courage enough, even at so tender an age, if we could have found the means to proceed; but our greatest difficulty seemed to be our father and mother.
>
> It astonished us greatly to find it said in what we were reading that pain and bliss were everlasting. We happened very often to talk about this; and we had a pleasure in repeating frequently, 'For ever, ever, ever.' Through the constant uttering of these words, our Lord was pleased that I should receive an abiding impression of the way of truth when I was yet a child.

Second, Teresa's most famous ecstatic experience, in a translation of 1642 that Crashaw might well have read:

> It pleased our Blessed Lord, that I should have sometimes, this following Vision. I saw an Angell very near me, towards my left side, and he appeared to me, in a Corporeall forme; though yet I am not wont to see anie thing of that kind, but very rarely. But, in this Vision, our Lord was pleased, that I should see this Angell, after this other manner. He was not great; but rather little; yet withall, he was of very much beautie. His face was so inflamed, that he appeared to be of those most Superior Angells, who seem to be, all in a fire; and he well might be of them, whome we call *Seraphins*; but as for me, they never tell me their names, or rankes; yet howsoever, I see thereby, that there is so great a difference in

Heaven, between one Angell, and another, as I am no way able to expresse. I saw, that he had a long Dart of gold in his hand; and at the end of the iron below, me thought, there was a little fire; and I conceaved, that he thrust it, some severall times, through my verie Hart, after such a manner, as that it passed the verie inwards, of my Bowells; and when he drew it back, me thought, it carried away, as much, as it had touched within me; and left all that, which remained, wholy inflamed with a great love of Almightye God. The paine of it, was so excessive, that it forced me to utter those groanes; and the suavitie, which that extremitie of paine gave, was also so very excessive, that there was no desiring at all, to be ridd of it; nor can the Soule then, receave anie contentment at all, in lesse, then God Almightie himself.

No apology for excluding *An Apologie for the fore-giving Hymne, as having been writ when the author was yet among the protestantes*! It is a flat special-pleading desert of logic-chopping after the Hymn's soaring flights and chalorous love-deaths (though see Sophie Read's eloquent defence of the thing's intellectual interest if not artistic value in ch. 4 of her book). Nor for omitting all but the close of *The Flaming Heart*, upon the 'seraphicall Saint's' book and picture, wherein overwrought paradoxes are twisted with barren ingenuity into a mixture that can only detract from the *Hymn*, here burnt-out and fanned in vain for fresh flames. The notion of a 'Teresa Trilogy', factitious at best, is at worst damaging to the poet's qualities, howsoever he himself might have conceived it. However I do concur with the consensus view that the 16 additional lines at the close, appended later, transport the poem to the level of the primal *Hymn*. Actually, inspiration begins to quicken rather before, at the paragraph commencing 'Leave her that...': the paradoxes kindle, the imperatives dig in, and the additional close comes as climactic continuation not total surprise. Even so there are a further twelve weak lines soon after that spoil this succession, which have to go.

Ambiguities again melt away with the *Hymn on the Assumption*, one of Crashaw's three greatest triumphs, a ravishing fantasia upon the *Song of Songs*. '*Echt*', as Pound would say (though never of this poet). Not perfect, however: it tails off slightly after its lyric climax, commands to 'come away' voiced by all Nature's generative/seasonal/gravitational urges culminating in Heaven's own Imperative in line 36. But unlike comparable cases, there would be compunction in cutting this one short, with its lithe command of highly variable line-lengths and exquisite control of rhythm and movement, local and overall. (And the closing 30-odd lines are not half bad by any other standards.)

Between the two main selections of sacred verse comes the second *intermezzo*. It starts with a selection of Crashaw's sacred epigrams, a few in English, mainly in Latin. This is just the tip of a flaming iceberg – the universal European culture, almost wholly lost to a modern readership, of Latin poetry (Greek too, less frequent), more widely disseminated and admired than work in living vernacular languages. The brilliance of Crashaw's epigrams was generally recognised: their manipulative neatness and extreme cleverness are as alien to nowadays as, for the most part, their subject matter and its lurid treatment, centred upon blood, flesh, wounds, tears, sucking and suckling, devouring and ingesting. But a selection wouldn't be complete without some kind of representation of this crucial aspect of his output. Here my ignorance has been guided by the knowledge of others. I can choose the English: the Latin has been advised by Alex Wong, who has also contributed the skilful literal translations through which the Latin can be easily followed. Sometimes there is also the poet's own vernacular version of his own original, facilitating a triple comparison.

Now a gathering of sacred fragments – crumbs from under the table. One piece of some length (*Quaerit Jesum suuam Maria*) is given complete, for its unusual rhythm and metre. Then some excerpts of beauty from poems pedestrian in the whole – *Out of Grotius his Tragedy of Christes Sufferinges*, eight lines wherein Jesus' reproaches turn to the miracle of the Wedding at Cana; and two longer stretches from a dedicatory piece accompanying the gift of a prayer-book: finally an eight-line gem of epigrammatic epitome.

The *intermezzo* ends with a second encounter between Crashaw and Cowley. My selection as a whole is prefaced by the finest lines in Cowley's loving but uneven *Elegy* for his older friend, and the first *intermezzo* contained Crashaw's gift to his precocious junior of a couple of green apricots. Their exchange here has a nobler subject – *Hope* – over whom they spar in a high-humoured agon not without aggro. The later text is preferred; but I've reverted to the earlier layout because it alternates the stanze, showing how the two contestants interlock closely in witty yet penetrating argument and counter-argument. The later edition prints Cowley complete and continuous, then Crashaw ditto, thus rather losing sight, literally, of the occasion and the point. Undoubtedly the victory is Crashaw's, in two unbroken closing stanze containing some of his most unstrained and unrestrained exuberance. Unwontedly staccato in this supremely legato writer – the monosyllables patter like hail: but the writing throughout is choice, charged with imagery at once gay, preposterous, and ravishingly lovely. Also *daring*: the passage culminating in

Hope's chast stealth harmes no more joyes maidenhead
Then spousall rites prejudge the marriage bed

is saucier than anywhere else in his work, sacred and secular. No sublimation here!

Cowley's much later backtracking *For Hope*, from *The Mistress* (1668), closes their reciprocal amity: no great shakes – a posthumous greeting to the fellow-artist more tenderly memorialised in the *Elegy*.

Finally, a selection from *Carmen Deo Nostro*, which appeared posthumously in Paris, 1652: 'containing some important matter never before published, but consisting chiefly of poems either first printed in 1648 or first printed there in their altered and expanded form' (L.C. Martin). The *Hymn* on the *Name of Jesus* is the longest of all such ode-like pieces except the cantata-like *Epiphany*-hymn; the most sustainedly resplendent though not the most profound, with much play of perfumes, roses, wings, honey, tears, joys, nests, doves: *ad infinitum* but not *ad nauseam* – there's a frisky freshness to it, and a play of line-length second to none. I have unashamedly made some cuts in *Charitas Nimia*, a poignant litany of shame and compunction turning what Empson would call the merely squalid imagery of payment/blackmail/redemption into something both plangent and spiritually searching. (What's omitted seems to me, perhaps presumptuously, to cheapen the balance of 'the dear bargain' elsewhere so delicately poised: it's also somewhat on the look-at-me-how-clever side, like the epigrams at their least convincing, yielding more hostages to hostility.)

Adoro Te, translated from Thomas Aquinas, is given as just one specimen, possibly the best, from a succession of translations, with free descanting, from the Latin and Italian; none is supreme, several give excessive opening for mockery or *déploration* (most notably the version of the *Stabat Mater*, most notoriously the deplorable version of the *Dies Irae*, both of them subjects and texts where one would expect Crashaw to excel). *To the same party, councel concerning her choice*, needs explanation: it's the sequel to the Hymn sent to a young gentlewoman with a little prayer-book excerpted earlier, where it was congruent with the commendation of Herbert's *Temple* and the *Wishes* to the Platonic female soulmate, placed here so late because of the clear anticipation of Crashaw's last poem, last also in this choice, in its language of urgent yet tender exhortation. The *Song* is an exquisite 'fluted' epitome of his principal themes in his most characteristic vocabulary – the amorous/ascetic paradoxes – 'living death and dying life'; 'dead to myself I live in thee' – posed without provocation as something utterly clear and simple.

The *Description of a Religious House*, taken from the Latin of John Barclay (1582–1621) is a precious bloom, in its perfect fusion of Crashaw's frugal aspect – naught too hot within – and the luscious love-deaths of his Teresa/Magdalen aspect, palpably eschewing the latter as it moves from the almost Pope-ian luxury in the opening eight lines (you expect to see a gaping triton at every turn), to unshorn woods, homely fare, coarse garments, still-returning pains, of the religious condition of life. I've dared omit five lines that (un)arguably mar this otherwise consistent piece. One low word is changed for another – *but* to *and*; the sense runs unbroken; the gem is flawless.

The expanded and enhanced version of the *Letter* to the Countess of Denbigh that came out separately and inexplicably even after its shorter, not so fine first appearance in the already posthumous *Carmen Deo Nostro* is of course preferred. The lover's traditional plea to maidens to make much of time, to the coy mistress to suffer herself to be desired, never more delicately, beautifully, fantastically uttered than here, crossed with the husbandman's plea for propagation and fruition – go forth and multiply – fuse wholly into the religious imperative, with persuasion now sweet and flirtatious, whimsical and reproachful, now seductive, now admonishing and urgent, now burning with the compunction and shame that failure to fulfil would entail, finally strong and forceful even unto ferocity in its paradoxes and commands: one of the great poems of the language, and of the world.

On the Death of Mr. Crashaw
(Abraham Cowley)

Poet and *Saint*! To thee alone are given
The two most sacred *Names* of *Earth* and *Heaven*.
The hard and rarest *Union* which can be
Next that of *Godhead* with *Humanitie*.

Ah wretched *We, Poets* of *Earth*! But *Thou*
Wert *Living* the same *Poet* which thou'rt *Now*.
Whilst *Angels* sing to thee their ayres divine,
And joy in an applause so great as *thine*.
Equal society with them to hold,
Thou need'st not make *new Songs*, but say the *Old*.
And they (kind Spirits!) shall all rejoice to see
How little less then *They, Exalted Man* may be.

Thy spotless *Muse*, like *Mary*, did contain
The boundless *Godhead*; she did well disdain
That her *eternal Verse* employ'd should be
On a less subject then *Eternitie*;
And for a sacred *Mistress* scorn'd to take,
But her whom *God* himself scorn'd not his *Spouse* to make.
It (in a kind) *her Miracle* did do;
A fruitful *Mother* was, and *Virgin* too.

* How well (blest Swan) did Fate contrive thy death;
And made thee render up thy tuneful breath
In thy great *Mistress* Arms? thou most divine
And richest *Off'ring* of *Loretto's Shrine*!
Where like some holy *Sacrifice* t'expire,
A *Fever* burns thee, and *Love* lights the *Fire*.
Angels (they say) brought the fam'ed *Chappel* there,
And bore the sacred Load in Triumph through the air.
'Tis surer much they brought thee there, and *They*,
And *Thou*, their charge, went *singing* all the way.

His *Faith* perhaps in some nice Tenents might
Be wrong; his *Life*, I'm sure, was *in the right*.
And I my self a *Catholick* will be,
So far at least, great *Saint*, to *Pray* to thee.

Lo here I beg (I whom thou once didst prove
So humble to *Esteem*, so Good to *Love*)
Not that thy *Spirit* might on me *Doubled* be,
I ask but *Half* thy mighty *Spirit* for Me.
And when my *Muse* soars with so strong a Wing,
'Twill learn of things *Divine*, and first of *Thee* to sing.

---

*   M. *Crashaw* died of a Fever at *Loretto*, being newly chosen Canon of that Church.

2

I
Secular

Musicks Duell

Now Westward *Sol* had spent the richest Beames
Of Noons high Glory, when hard by the streams
Of *Tiber*, on the sceane of a greene plat,
Under protection of an Oake; there sate
A sweet Lutes-master: in whose gentle aires
Hee lost the Dayes heat, and his owne hot cares.
  Close in the covert of the leaves there stood
A Nightingale, come from the neighbouring wood:
(The sweet inhabitant of each glad Tree,
Their Muse, their *Syren*. harmlesse *Syren* shee)   10
There stood she listning, and did entertaine
The Musicks soft report: and mold the same
In her owne murmures, that what ever mood
His curious fingers lent, her voyce made good:
The man perceiv'd his Rivall, and her Art,
Dispos'd to give the light-foot Lady sport
Awakes his Lute, and 'gainst the fight to come
Informes it, in a sweet *Præludium*
Of closer straines, and ere the warre begin,
Hee lightly skirmishes on every string   20
Charg'd with a flying touch: and streightway shee
Carves out her dainty voyce as readily,
Into a thousand sweet distinguish'd Tones,
And reckons up in soft divisions,
Quicke volumes of wild Notes; to let him know
By that shrill taste, shee could doe something too.
  His nimble hands instinct then taught each string
A capring cheerefullnesse; and made them sing
To their owne dance; now negligently rash
Hee throwes his Arme, and with a long drawne dash   30
Blends all together; then distinctly tripps
From this to that; then quicke returning skipps
And snatches this againe, and pauses there.
Shee measures every measure, every where
Meets art with art; sometimes as if in doubt
Not perfect yet, and fearing to bee out
Trayles her playne Ditty in one long-spun note,
Through the sleeke passage of her open throat:

5

A cleare unwrinckled song, then doth shee point it
With tender accents, and severely joynt it   40
By short diminutives, that being rear'd
In controverting warbles evenly shar'd,
With her sweet selfe shee wrangles; Hee amazed
That from so small a channell should be rais'd
The torrent of a voyce, whose melody
Could melt into such sweet variety
Straines higher yet; that tickled with rare art
The tatling strings (each breathing in his part)
Most kindly doe fall out; the grumbling Base
In surly groanes disdaines the Trebles Grace.   50
The high-perch't treble chirps at this, and chides,
Untill his finger (Moderatour) hides
And closes the sweet quarrell, rowsing all
Hoarce, shrill, at once; as when the Trumpets call
Hot Mars to th' Harvest of Deaths field, and woo
Mens hearts into their hands; this lesson too
Shee gives him backe; her supple Brest thrills out
Sharpe Aires, and staggers in a warbling doubt
Of dallying sweetnesse, hovers ore her skill,
And folds in wav'd notes with a trembling bill,   60
The plyant Series of her slippery song.
Then starts shee suddenly into a Throng
Of short thicke sobs, whose thundring volleyes float,
And roule themselves over her lubricke throat
In panting murmurs, still'd out of her Breast
That ever-bubling spring; the sugred Nest
Of her delicious soule, that there does lye
Bathing in streames of liquid Melodie;
Musicks best seed-plot, whence in ripend Aires
A Golden-headed Harvest fairely reares   70
His Honey-dropping tops, plow'd by her breath
Which there reciprocally laboureth
In that sweet soyle. It seemes a holy quire
Founded to th' Name of great *Apollo's* lyre.
Whose sylver-roofe rings with the sprightly notes
Of sweet-lipp'd Angell-Imps, that swill their throats
In creame of Morning *Helicon,* and then
Preferre soft Anthems to the Eares of men,
To woo them from their Beds, still murmuring

That men can sleepe while they their Mattens sing: 80
(Most divine service) whose so early lay,
Prevents the Eye-lidds of the blushing day.
There might you heare her kindle her soft voyce,
In the close murmur of a sparkling noyse.
And lay the ground-worke of her hopefull song,
Still keeping in the forward streame, so long
Till a sweet whirle-wind (striving to gett out)
Heaves her soft Bosome, wanders round about,
And makes a pretty Earthquake in her Breast,
Till the fledg'd Notes at length forsake their Nest;   90
Fluttering in wanton shoales, and to the Sky
Wing'd with their owne wild Eccho's pratling fly.
Shee opes the floodgate, and lets loose a Tide
Of streaming sweetnesse, which in state doth ride
On the wav'd backe of every swelling straine,
Rising and falling in a pompous traine.
And while shee thus discharges a shrill peale
Of flashing Aires; shee qualifies their zeale
With the coole Epode of a graver Noat,
Thus high, thus low, as if her silver throat   100
Would reach the brasen voyce of warr's hoarce Bird;
Her little soule is ravisht: and so pour'd
Into loose extasies, that shee is plac't
Above her selfe, Musicks *Enthusiast.*
  Shame now and anger mixt a double staine
In the Musitians face; yet once againe
(Mistresse) I come; now reach a straine my Lute
Above her mocke, or bee for ever mute.
Or tune a song of victory to mee,
Or to thy selfe, sing thine owne Obsequie;   110
So said, his hands sprightly as fire hee flings,
And with a quavering coynesse tasts the strings.
The sweet-lip't sisters musically frighted,
Singing their feares are fearfully delighted.
Trembling as when *Appollo's* golden haires
Are fan'd and frizled, in the wanton ayres
Of his owne breath: which marryed to his lyre
Doth tune the *Sphæares,* and make Heavens selfe looke higher.
From this to that, from that to this hee flyes
Feeles Musicks pulse in all her Arteryes,   120

7

Caught in a net which there *Appollo* spreads,
His fingers struggle with the vocall threads,
Following those little rills, hee sinkes into
A Sea of *Helicon;* his hand does goe
Those parts of sweetnesse which with *Nectar* drop,
Softer then that which pants in *Hebe's* cup.
The humourous strings expound his learned touch,
By various Glosses; now they seeme to grutch,
And murmur in a buzzing dinne, then gingle
In shrill tongu'd accents: striving to bee single.   130
Every smooth turne, every delicious stroake
Gives life to some new Grace; thus doth h'invoke
Sweetnesse by all her Names; thus, bravely thus
(Fraught with a fury so harmonious)
The Lutes light *Genius* now does proudly rise,
Heav'd on the surges of swolne Rapsodyes.
Whose flourish (Meteor-like) doth curle the aire
With flash of high-borne fancyes: here and there
Dancing in lofty measures, and anon
Creeps on the soft touch of a tender tone: 140
Whose trembling murmurs melting in wild aires
Runs to and fro, complaining his sweet cares
Because those pretious mysteryes that dwell,
In musick's ravish't soule hee dare not tell,
But whisper to the world: thus doe they vary
Each string his Note, as if they meant to carry
Their Masters blest soule (snatcht out at his Eares
By a strong Extasy) through all the sphæares
Of Musicks heaven; and seat it there on high
In th' *Empyræum* of pure Harmony.   150
At length (after so long, so loud a strife
Of all the strings, still breathing the best life
Of blest variety attending on
His fingers fairest revolution
In many a sweet rise, many as sweet a fall)
A full-mouth *Diapason* swallowes all.
   This done, hee lists what shee would say to this,
And shee although her Breath's late exercise
Had dealt too roughly with her tender throate,
Yet summons all her sweet powers for a Noate   160
Alas! in vaine! for while (sweet soule) shee tryes

8

To measure all those wild diversities
Of chatt'ring stringes, by the small size of one
Poore simple voyce, rais'd in a Naturall Tone;
Shee failes, and failing grieves, and grieving dyes.
Shee dyes; and leaves her life the Victors prise,
Falling upon his Lute; ô fit to have
(That liv'd so sweetly) dead, so sweet a Grave!

In praise of Lessius
his rule of health

Goe now with some dareing drugg,
Baite thy disease, and while they tugg
Thou to maintaine their cruell strife,
Spend the deare treasure of thy life:
Goe take phisicke, doat upon
Some bigg-named composition,
The oraculous doctors mistick bills,
Certain hard words made into pills;
And what at length shalt get by these?
Onely a costlyer disease.   10
Goe poore man thinke what shall bee,
Remedie against thy remedie.
That which makes us have no need
Of Phisick thats Phisick indeed.
  Harke hether, Reader, wouldst thou see
Nature her owne Physitian bee.
Wouldst see a man all, his owne wealth,
His owne Physick, his owne health?
A man whose sober soule can tell,
How to weare her garments well?   20
Her garments that upon her sit,
As garments should doe close and fit?
A well cloathed soule thats not opprest,
Nor choakt with what shee should bee drest?
A soule sheathed in a christall shrine,
Through which all her bright features shine?
As when a peece of wanton lawne,
A thinne aiereall vaile is drawne
O're beauties face, seeming to hide
More sweetly showes the blushing bride.   30
A soule whose intelectuall beames
No mistes doe maske no lazy steames?
A happy soule that all the way,
To heaven, hath a summers day?
Would'st thou see a man whose well warmed blood,
Bathes him in a genuine flood?

A man whose tuned humours bee,
A set of rarest harmony?
Wouldst see blith lookes, fresh cheeks beguile
Age, wouldst see *December* smile? 40
Wouldst see a nest of Roses grow
In a bed of reverend snow?
Warme thoughts free spirits, flattering
Winters selfe into a spring?
In summe, wouldst see a man that can
Live to bee old and still a man?

Epithalamium

1.   Come virgin Tapers of pure waxe
      made in the Hive of Love, all white
as snow, and yet as cold, where lackes
    Hymens holy heate and light;
      where blooming kisses
        their beds yet keepe
      and steepe their blisses
        in Rosy sleepe;
where sister budds yet wanting brothers
kisse their owne lipps in Lieu of others;   10
helpe me to mourne a matchlesse maydenhead
        that now is dead:

2.   A fine thinn negative thing it was,
      a nothing with a dainty name,
which pruned her plumes in selfe loves glasse,
    made up of fancy and fond fame;
      within the shade
        of its owne winge
      it sate and played
        a selfe crownd King;   20
A froward flower, whose peevish pride
within it selfe, it selfe did hide,
flying all fingers, and even thinking much
        of its owne touch:

3.   This bird indeed the phænix was
      late chaced by loves revengefull arrowes,
whose warres now left the wonted passe
    and spared the litle lives of sparrowes;
      to hunt this foole
        whose froward pride,   30
      Loves noble schoole,
        and Courts denyed,
And froze the fruite of faire desire
which flourisheth in mutuall fire,
'gainst nature, who 'mong all the webbs she spunn
        nere wove A Nunne:

4.   She of Cupids shafts afraid
      left her owne balme-breathing East,
    and in a westerne bosome made
      a softer, and a sweeter neast;   40
        there did she rest
          in the sweet shade,
        of a soft breast,
          whose beauties made
    Thames oft stand still, and lend a glasse
    while in her owne she saw heavens face,
    and sent him full of her faire names report
          to Thetis Court

5.   And now poore Love was at a stand
      the Christall castle which she kept   50
    was proofe against the proudest hand;
      there in safest hold she slept
        his shafts expence
          left there noe smart,
        but bounding thence
          broached his owne heart;
    At length a fort he did devise
    built in noble Brampstons eyes
    and ayming thence this matchlesse maydenhead
          was soone found dead: 60

6.   Yet Love in death did wayte upon her,
      granting leave she should expire
    in her fumes, and have the honour
      t' exhale in flames of his owne fire;
        her funerall pyle
          the marriage bedd,
        in a sighed smile
          she vanished.
    So rich a dresse of death nere famed
    the Cradles where her kindred flamed;   70
    so sweet her mother phænixes of th' East
          nere spiced their neast:

7.   With many pretty peevish tryalls
      of angry yeelding, faint denyings,

13

melting No's, and milde denyalls,
  dying lives, and short lived dyings;
    with doubtfull eyes,
      halfe smiles, halfe teares,
    with trembling joyes,
      and jocund feares;   80
Twixt the pretty twylight strife
of dying maide and dawning wife;
twixt raine, and sun-shine, this sweet maydenhead
      alas is dead:

8.   Happy he whose wakefull joyes
    kept the prize of this rich losse,
happy she whose watry eyes
    kisse noe worse a weeping Crosse;
      thrice happy he
        partakes her store,   90
      thrice happy she
        hath still the more.
Thinke not sweet Bride, that faint shewer slakes
the fires he from thy faire eyes takes,
Thy dropps are salt, and while they thinke to tame,
      sharpen his flame:

9.   Blessd Bridegroome ere the raine be layd
    use good weather while it proves,
those dropps that wash away the maide
    shall water your warme planted loves;   100
      faire youth make haste
        ere it be drye
      the sweet brine taste
        from her moist eye;
Thy lipps will finde such deaw as this is
best season for a lovers kisses,
and those thy morning starres will better please
      bathed in those seas:

10.   Nor may thy Vine, faire oake, embrace thee
    with ivy armes, and empty wishes,   110
but with full bosome enterlace thee,
    and reach her Clusters to thy kisses;

safe may she rest
    her laden boughes,
on thy firme breast,
    and fill thy vowes,
up to the brimm, till she make even
their full topps with the faire eyed heaven,
And heaven to guild those glorious Hero's birth
        stoope and kisse earth: 120

11.   Long may this happy heaven tyed band
      exercise its most holy art,
keeping her heart within his hand,
    keeping his hand upon her heart,
      but from her eyes
        feele he noe Charmes,
      finde she noe joy
        but in his armes;
May each maintaine a well fledged neast
of winged loves in eithers breast,   130
Be each of them a mutuall sacrifice
        of eithers eyes:

12.   May their whole life a sweet song prove
      sett to two well composed parts,
by musickes noblest master, Love,
    playd on the strings of both their harts;
      whose mutuall sound
        may ever meete
      in a just round,
        not short though sweet;   140
Long may heaven listen to the songe,
and thinke it short though it bee long;
oh prove't a well sett song indeed, which showes
        sweet'st in the Close.

Upon the Kings coronation

Sound forth, cælestiall Organs, lett heavens quire
Ravish the dancing orbes, make them mount higher
With nimble capers, & force Atlas tread
Upon his tiptoes, e're his silver head
Shall kisse his golden burthen. Thou, glad Isle,
That swim'st as deepe in joy, as Seas, now smile;
Lett not thy weighty glories, this full tide
Of blisse, debase thee; but with a just pride
Swell: swell to such an height, that thou maist vye
With heaven itselfe for stately Majesty.   10
Doe not deceive mee, Eyes: doe I not see
In this blest earth heavens bright Epitome,
Circled with pure refined glory? heere
I veiw a rising sunne in this our sphære,
Whose blazing beames, maugre the blackest night,
And mists of greife, dare force a joyfull light.
The gold, in wch he flames, does well præsage
A precious season, & a golden age.
Doe I not see joy keepe his revels now,
And sitt triumphing in each cheerfull brow?   20
Unmixt felicity with silver wings
Broodeth this sacred place. hither peace brings
The choicest of her olive-crownes, & praies
To have them guilded with his courteous raies.
Doe I not see a Cynthia, who may
Abash the purest beauties of the day?
To whom heavens lampes often in silent night
Steale from their stations to repaire their light.
Doe I not see a constellation,
Each little beame of wch would make a sunne?   30
I meane those three great starres, who well may scorne
Acquaintance with the Usher of the morne.
To gaze upon such starres each humble eye
Would be ambitious of Astronomie.
Who would not be a Phænix, & aspire
To sacrifice himselfe in such sweet fire?
Shine forth, ye flaming sparkes of Deity,
Yee perfect Emblemes of Divinity.

16

Fixt in your sphæres of glory, shed from thence
The treasures of our lives, your influence.   40
For if you sett, who may not justly feare,
The world will be one Ocean, one great teare.

On a foule Morning, being then to take a journey

Where art thou Sol, while thus the blind-fold Day
Staggers out of the East, looses her way
Stumbling on Night? Rouze thee Illustrious Youth,
And let no dull mists choake the Lights faire growth.
Point here thy Beames; ô glance on yonder flockes,
And make their fleeces Golden as thy lockes.
Unfold thy faire front, and there shall appeare
Full glory, flaming in her owne free spheare.
Gladnesse shall cloath the Earth, we will instile
The face of things, an universall smile.   10
Say to the Sullen Morne, thou com'st to court her;
And wilt command proud *Zephirus* to sport her
With wanton gales: his balmy breath shall licke
The tender drops which tremble on her cheeke;
Which rarifyed, and in a gentle raine
On those delicious bankes distill'd againe
Shall rise in a sweet Harvest; which discloses
Two ever blushing beds of new-borne Roses.
Hee'l fan her bright locks teaching them to flow,
And friske in curl'd *Mæanders*: Hee will throw   20
A fragrant Breath suckt from the spicy nest
O'th pretious *Phœnix*, warme upon her Breast.
Hee with a dainty and soft hand, will trim
And brush her Azure Mantle, which shall swim
In silken Volumes; wheresoe're shee'l tread,
Bright clouds like Golden fleeces shall be spread.
  Rise then (faire blew-ey'd Maid) rise and discover
Thy silver brow, and meet thy Golden lover.
See how hee runs, with what a hasty flight
Into thy Bosome, bath'd with liquid Light.   30
Fly, fly prophane fogs, farre hence fly away,
Taint not the pure streames of the springing Day,
With your dull influence, it is for you,
To sit and scoule upon Nights heavy brow;
Not on the fresh cheekes of the virgin Morne,
Where nought but smiles, and ruddy joyes are worne.
Fly then, and doe not thinke with her to stay;
Let it suffice, shee'l weare no maske to day.

On Marriage

I Would be married, but I'd have no Wife,
I Would be married to a single Life.

An Epitaph upon a Young Married Couple Dead and Buried Together

To these, whom DEATH again did wed,
This GRAVE's their second Marriage-bed.
For though the hand of fate could force
'Twixt SOUL & BODY a Divorce,
It could not sunder man & WIFE,
'Cause They Both lived but one life.
Peace, good Reader. Doe not weep.
Peace, The Lovers are asleep.
They, sweet Turtles, folded ly
In the last knott love could ty.   10
And though they ly as they were dead,
Their Pillow stone, their sheetes of lead,
(Pillow hard, & sheetes not warm)
Love made the bed; They'l take no harm
Let them sleep: let them sleep on.
Till this stormy night be gone,
Till the' Æternall morrow dawn;
Then the curtaines will be drawn
And they wake into a light,
Whose day shall neuer dy in Night.   20

The Authors Motto

Live Jesus, Live, and let it bee
My life to dye, for love of thee.

19

Wishes
To his (Supposed) Mistresse

Who ere shee bee,
That not impossible shee
That shall command my heart and mee;

Where ere shee lye,
Lock't up from mortall Eye,
In shady leaves of Destiny:

Till that ripe Birth
Of studied fate stand forth,
And teach her faire steps to our Earth;

Till that Divine   10
Idæa, take a shrine
Of Chrystall flesh, through which to shine:

Meet you her my wishes,
Bespeake her to my blisses,
And bee yee call'd my absent kisses.

I wish her Beauty,
That owes not all his Duty
To gaudy Tire, or glistring shoo-ty.

Something more than
Taffata or Tissew can,   20
Or rampant feather, or rich fan.

More then the spoyle
Of shop, or silkewormes Toyle
Or a bought blush, or a set smile.

A face thats best
By its owne beauty drest,
And can alone commend the rest.

A face made up
Out of no other shop,
Then what natures white hand sets ope.   30

A cheeke where Youth,
And Blood, with Pen of Truth
Write, what the Reader sweetly ru'th.

A Cheeke where growes
More then a Morning Rose:
Which to no Boxe his being owes.

Lipps, where all Day
A lovers kisse may play,
Yet carry nothing thence away.

Lookes that oppresse   40
Their richest Tires but dresse
And cloath their simplest Nakednesse.

Eyes, that displaces
The Neighbour Diamond, and out faces
That Sunshine by their owne sweet Graces.

Tresses, that weare
Jewells, but to declare
How much themselves more pretious are.

Whose native Ray,
Can tame the wanton Day   50
Of Gems, that in their bright shades play.

Each Ruby there,
Or Pearle that dare appeare,
Bee its owne blush, bee its owne Teare.

A well tam'd Heart,
For whose more noble smart,
Love may bee long chusing a Dart.

Eyes, that bestow
Full quivers on loves Bow;
Yet pay lesse Arrowes then they owe.   60

Smiles, that can warme
The blood, yet teach a charme,
That Chastity shall take no harme.

Blushes, that bin
The burnish of no sin,
Nor flames of ought too hot within.

Joyes, that confesse,
Vertue their Mistresse,
And have no other head to dresse.

Feares, fond and flight,   70
As the coy Brides, when Night
First does the longing lover right.

Teares, quickly fled,
And vaine, as those are shed
For a dying Maydenhead.

Dayes, that need borrow,
No part of their good Morrow,
From a fore spent night of sorrow.

Dayes, that in spight
Of Darkenesse, by the Light   80
Of a cleere mind are Day all Night.

Nights, sweet as they,
Made short by lovers play,
Yet long by th'absence of the Day.

Life, that dares send
A challenge to his end,
And when it comes say *Welcome Friend*.

Sydnæan showers
Of sweet discourse, whose powers
Can Crowne old Winters head with flowers,   90

Soft silken Houres,
Open sunnes; shady Bowers,
Bove all; Nothing within that lowres.

What ere Delight
Can make Dayes forehead bright;
Or give Downe to the Wings of Night.

In her whole frame,
Have Nature all the Name,
Art and ornament the shame.

Her flattery,   100
Picture and Poesy,
Her counsell her owne vertue bee.

I wish, her store
Of worth, may leave her poore
Of wishes; And I wish —— No more.

Now if Time knowes
That her whose radiant Browes,
Weave them a Garland of my vowes;

Her whose just Bayes,
My future hopes can raise,   110
A trophie to her present praise;

Her that dares bee,
What these Lines wish to see
I seeke no further, it is shee.

'Tis shee, and heere
Lo I uncloath and cleare,
My wishes cloudy Character.

May shee enjoy it,
Whose merit dare apply it,
But Modesty dares still deny it.

Such worth as this is,
Shall fixe my flying wishes,
And determine them to kisses.

Let her full Glory,
My fancyes, fly before yee,
Bee ye my fictions; But her story.

Intermezzo I

Upon two greene Apricockes sent to Cowley
by Sir Crashaw

Take these, times tardy truants, sent by me,
To be chastis'd (sweet friend) and chidd by thee.
Pale sons of our *Pomona*! whose wan cheekes
Have spent the patience of expecting weekes,
Yet are scarce ripe enough at best to show
The redd, but of the blush to thee they ow.
By thy comparrison they shall put on
More summer in their shames reflection,
Than ere the fruitfull *Phæbus* flaming kisses
Kindled on their cold lips. O had my wishes   10
And the deare merits of your Muse, their due,
The yeare had found some fruit early as you;
Ripe as those rich composures time computes
Blossoms, but our blest tast confesses fruits.
How does thy April-Autumne mocke these cold
Progressions 'twixt whose termes poor time grows old?
With thee alone he weares no beard, thy braine
Gives him the morning worlds fresh gold againe.
'Twas only Paradice, 'tis onely thou,
Whose fruit and blossoms both blesse the same bough.   20
Proud in the patterne of thy pretious youth,
Nature (methinks) might easily mend her growth.
Could she in all her births but coppie thee,
Into the publick yeares proficiencie,
No fruit should have the face to smile on thee
(Young master of the worlds maturitie)
But such whose sun-borne beauties what they borrow
Of beames to day, pay back againe to morrow,
Nor need be double-gilt. How then must these,
Poore fruites looke pale at thy Hesperides!   30
Faine would I chide their slownesse, but in their
Defects I draw mine owne dull character.
Take them, and me in them acknowledging,
How much my summer waites upon thy spring.

On Mr. G. Herberts booke intituled the Temple of Sacred Poems, sent to a Gentlewoman

Know you faire, on what you looke;
Divinest love lyes in this booke:
Expecting fire from your eyes,
To kindle this his sacrifice.
When your hands unty these strings,
Thinke you have an Angell by th' wings.
One that gladly will bee nigh,
To wait upon each morning sigh.
To flutter in the balmy aire,
Of your well perfumed prayer.   10
These white plumes of his heele lend you,
Which every day to heaven will send you:
To take acquaintance of the spheare,
And all the smooth faced kindred there.
And though *Herberts* name doe owe
These devotions, fairest; know
That while I lay them on the shrine
Of your white hand, they are mine.

College Elegies
(selections, mostly excerpted)

Upon the Death of a Gentleman [Mr Chambers]

Faithlesse and fond Mortality,
Who will ever credit thee?
Fond and faithlesse thing! that thus,
In our best hopes beguilest us.
What a reckoning hast thou made,
Of the hopes in him we laid?
For Life by volumes lengthened,
A Line or two, to speake him dead.
For the Laurell in his verse,
The sullen Cypresse o're his Herse.   10
For a silver-crowned Head,
A durty pillow in Death's Bed.
For so deare, so deep a trust,
Sad requitall, thus much dust!
Now though the blow that snatcht him hence,
Stopt the Mouth of Eloquence,
Though shee be dumbe e're since his Death,
Not us'd to speake but in his Breath,
Yet if at least shee not denyes,
The sad language of our eyes,   20
Wee are contented: for then this
Language none more fluent is.
Nothing speakes our Griefe so well
As to speake Nothing, Come then tell
Thy mind in Teares who e're Thou be,
That ow'st a Name to misery.
Eyes are vocall, Teares have Tongues,
And there be words not made with lungs;
Sententious showers, ô let them fall,
Their cadence is Rhetoricall.   30
Here's a Theame will drinke th'expence,
Of all thy watry Eloquence,
Weepe then, onely be exprest
Thus much, *Hee's Dead,* and weepe the rest.

from *Upon the Death of Mr. Herrys*

...The timourous Maiden-Blossomes on each Bough,
Peept forth from their first blushes: so that now
A Thousand ruddy hopes smil'd in each Bud,
And flatter'd every greedy eye that stood
Fixt in Delight, as if already there
Those rare fruits dangled, whence the Golden Yeare
His crowne expected, when (ô Fate, ô Time
That seldome lett'st a blushing youthfull Prime   30
Hide his hot Beames in shade of silver Age;
So rare is hoary vertue) the dire rage
Of a mad storme these bloomy joyes all tore,
Ravisht the Maiden Blossoms, and downe bore
The trunke. Yet in this Ground his pretious Root
Still lives, which when weake Time shall be pour'd out
Into Eternity, and circular joyes
Dance in an endlesse round, againe shall rise
The faire son of an ever-youthfull Spring,
To be a shade for Angels while they sing...   40

from *Upon the Death of the most desired Mr. Herrys*

...Spare him Death, ô spare him then,
Spare the sweetest among men.   60
Let not pitty with her Teares,
Keepe such distance from thine Eares.
But ô thou wilt not, canst not spare,
Haste hath never time to heare.
Therefore if hee needs must go,
And the Fates will have it so,
Softly may he be possest,
Of his monumentall rest.
Safe, thou darke home of the dead,
Safe ô hide his loved head.   70
For Pitties sake ô hide him quite,
From his Mother Natures sight:
Lest for Griefe his losse may move,
All her Births abortive prove.

from *His Epitaph*

…In him Goodnesse joy'd to see
Learning, learne Humility.
The splendor of his Birth and Blood,
Was but the Glosse of his owne Good:
The flourish of his sober Youth,
Was the Pride of Naked Truth.
In composure of his face,
Liv'd a faire, but manly Grace.
His Mouth was Rhetoricks best mold,
His Tongue the Touchstone of her Gold.   30
What word so e're his Breath kept warme,
Was no word now but a charme.
For all persuasive Graces thence
Suck't their sweetest Influence.
His vertue that within had root,
Could not chuse but shine without.
And th'heart-bred lustre of his worth,
At each corner peeping forth,
Pointed him out in all his wayes,
Circled round in his owne Rayes: 40
That to his sweetnesse, all mens eyes
Were vow'd Loves flaming Sacrifice.

from *An Elegy upon the death of Mr Stanninow fellow of Queenes Colledge*

'Twas not the frozen zone; One sparke of fire,
Shott from his flaming eye, had thaw'd it's ire,
And made it burne in love: 'Twas not the rage,
And too ungentle nippe of frosty age:
'Twas not the chast, & purer snow, whose nest
Was in the modest Nunnery of his brest:
Noe. none of these ravish't those virgin roses,
The Muses, & the Graces fragrant posies.
W^{ch}, while they smiling sate upon his face,
They often kist, & in the sugred place   40
Left many a starry teare, to thinke how soone
The golden harvest of our joyes, the noone

31

Of all our glorious hopes should fade,
And be eclipsed with an envious shade.
Noe. 'twas old doting Death, who, stealing by,
Dragging his crooked burthen, look't awry,
And streight his amorous syth (greedy of blisse)
Murdred the earth's just pride with a rude kisse...

On the death of Wm Henshaw, student in Eman. Coll.

See a sweet streame of Helicon,
Runne into death's black Ocean.
See his pretious silver wave
I' th' jetty channele of a grave.
Hither, Muses, turne your eyes,
See where your Aqua-vitæ lies.
Angry heaven doth now bequeath
This living fountaine unto death.
Come therefore now, & him interre,
Find him a glorious Sepulcher.   10
But trust him not unto the earth,
She had him ever since his birth.
In yor breasts lett him have roome,
In those snowy hills a tombe.
Come, weave your locks, those threads of gold,
Make a winding sheet, t'enfold
His Ivory limbs; & in this shrine,
Heavens milky way he shall outshine.
From the Alablaster banckes
Of your cheekes pluck all the ranckes   20
Of those modest blushing roses,
And the Lillies: make you posies,
To deck his hearse; & lett each wear
The liquid jewell of a teare.
Your starry eyes, like tapers, burne,
That may conduct us to his urne.
Where when our wat'ry eyes shall see
Our pictures of mortalitie,
There soe lovely, faire, & bright,
And soe sumptuously dight,   30
(Narcissus-like) wee'l flame in love,

And his funerall fewell prove.
For in this shape, that now Death is,
To entertaine him were a blisse.

   Attrib. P. Cornwallis, but all stylistic traits indicate Crashaw.

An Elegy upon the death of M[r] Christopher Rouse Esquire

  Christopher Rouse.
        } Anagr.
  Oh rich purest rose.

Rich, purest rose, prime flowre of blooming youth,
That once did'st flourish in a happy growth,
Soe sweetly loaden with perfumes, that low
The fragrant burthen made thy stalke to bow:
When amorous heav'en beheld it, straightway to it
Thousands of sacred Cupids came to woo it.
Like as I've seene the daily labouring Bee
Fly from her thatched cottage merrily
Unto some honyed mine, & all along
The way singing a plaine melodious song,   10
Spying at length the lillies snowy breasts,
Or the pure sanguine roses cheekes, she rests,
And Siren-like pleasantly sings a while,
Untill sh' hath flatter'd out her precious spoile,
Then to her waxen closets home she flies,
Bearing the liquid gold upon her thighes:
Just soe those heavenly Sirens, that doe swimme
In gulfes of deepest blisse, when they saw him,
Came singing divine Anthems, as they flew
Into the Paradise, where this rose grew.   20
Then on each part sate a cælestiall Bee,
That sung a sweet song for as sweet a fee;
Thus heaven with earth did traffick, they did buy
The purest sweetnes for pure harmony.
But at the length into their starry hive
They snatch't the rose itselfe; thus they deprive
Earth of its most delicious influence,
Of all perfumes the very Quintessence;
I meane that precious soule, where every Grace

Tooke upp its heaven on earth; that glorious place,   30
Where each faire Virgin-vertue had her throne,
Each her embalmed habitation.
This was the Muses Helicon, the blest
Parnassus, where each had a Phœnix nest.
This have they tooke, leaving the spoiled stemme,
I meane that corpes, the Caskett of that jemme,
W^{ch} earst wee had, sparkling with heavenly light,
With every starre of excellencie dight;
But now have lost. ô Sorrow, give me leave
To begg this boone of those, that did bereave   40
Us of our blisse, that from their wings soe bright
One golden quill may take an easy flight:
With wch these lines I may characterize
O're the blest place, where this rich relique lies.

from *Sospetto d'Herode*

The argument of Book I strangely pre-echoes some stretches of Paradise
Lost *– an expedition from 'Deaths Master' to earth, in order to thwart
Divine Designs by tempting Herod to massacre all newborn male infants
in his realm. Canti 5–9 evoke the infernal regions with many a snake, stink,
ever-consuming fire and gnashing of teeth. Recalling his primal quarrel
with Heaven, Satan sees new possibilities for mischief and revenge:*

13

Heavens Golden-winged Herald, late hee saw
To a poore *Galilean* virgin sent
How low the Bright Youth bow'd, and with what awe
Immortall flowers to her faire hand present.
Hee saw th'old *Hebrewes* wombe, neglect the Law
Of Age and Barennesse, and her Babe prevent
  His Birth, by his Devotion, who began
  Betimes to be a Saint, before a Man.

14

Hee saw rich Nectar thawes, release the rigour
Of th'Icy North, from frost-bcount *Atlas* hands
His Adamantine fetters fall: greene vigour
Gladding the *Scythian* Rocks, and *Libian* sands.
Hee saw a vernall smile, sweetly disfigure
Winters sad face, and through the flowry lands
  Of faire *Engaddi* hony-sweating Fountaines
  With *Manna*, Milk, and Balm, new broach the Mountaines.

15

Hee saw how in that blest Day-bearing Night,
The Heav'n-rebuked shades made hast away;
How bright a Dawne of Angels with new Light
Amaz'd the midnight world, and made a Day

Of which the Morning knew not: Mad with spight
Hee markt how the poore Shepheards ran to pay
  Their simple Tribute to the Babe, whose Birth
  Was the great businesse both of Heav'n and Earth.

16

Hee saw a threefold Sun, with rich encrease,
Make proud the Ruby portalls of the East.
Hee saw the Temple sacred to sweet Peace,
Adore her Princes Birth, flat on her Brest.
Hee saw the falling Idols, all confesse
A comming Deity. Hee saw the Nest
  Of pois'nous and unnaturall loves, Earth-nurst;
  Toucht with the worlds true *Antidote* to burst.

17

He saw Heav'n blossome with a new-borne light,
On which, as on a glorious stranger gaz'd
The Golden eyes of Night: whose Beame made bright
The way to *Beth'lem,* and as boldly blaz'd,
(Nor askt leave of the Sun) by Day as Night.
By whom (as Heav'ns illustrious Hand-maid) rais'd
  Three Kings (or what is more) three Wise men went
  Westward to find the worlds true Orient.

*The opportunity is too good to waste: a grand display of familiar paradoxes
– low/high; feeble/strong; virgin/mother; eternity/time (etc.) – is given a
characteristically Crashavian turn:*

21

But these vast Mysteries his senses smother,
And Reason (for what's Faith to him?) devoure.
How she that is a maid should prove a Mother,
Yet keepe inviolate her virgin flower;
How Gods eternall Sonne should be mans Brother,
Poseth his proudest Intellectuall power.

How a pure Spirit should incarnate bee,
And life it selfe weare Deaths fraile Livery.

22

That the Great Angell-blinding light should shrinke
His blaze, to shine in a poore Shepheards eye.
That the unmeasur'd God so low should sinke,
As Pris'ner in a few poore Rags to lye.
That from his Mothers Brest hee milke should drinke,
Who feeds with Nectar Heav'ns faire family.
  That a vile Manger his low Bed should prove,
  Who in a Throne of stars Thunders above.

23

That hee whom the Sun serves, should faintly peepe
Through clouds of Infant flesh: that hee the old
Eternall Word should bee a Child, and weepe.
That hee who made the fire, should feare the cold;
That Heav'ns high Majesty his Court should keepe
In a clay-cottage, by each blast control'd.
  That Glories selfe should serve our Griefs, & feares:
  And free Eternity, submit to yeares.

24

And further, that the Lawes eternall Giver,
Should bleed in his owne lawes obedience:
And to the circumcising Knife deliver
Himselfe, the forfeit of his slaves offence.
That the unblemisht Lambe, blessed for ever,
Should take the marke of sin, and paine of sence.
  These are the knotty Riddles, whose darke doubt
  Intangles his lost Thoughts, past getting out.

In the next seven stanze Satan speaks, or rather 'bellows' (canto 26) in his own direct voice. His minions reply with acclamation –

> Here thou art Lord alone
> Boundlesse and absolute: Hell is thine owne...

and the next stanza continues their counsel in vocabulary unmistakably Crashaw's:

35

If usuall wit, and strength will doe no good,
Vertues of stones, nor herbes: use stronger charmes,
Anger, and love, best hookes of humane blood.
If all faile wee'l put on our proudest Armes,
And pouring on Heav'ns face the Seas huge flood
Quench his curl'd fires, wee'l wake with our Alarmes
  Ruine, where e're she sleepes at Natures feet;
  And crush the world till his wide corners meet.

The infernal colloquy concludes with the choice of Cruelty, singled out from the 'cursed knot of Hags' to best insinuate the mooted crime. Her horrid palace is vividly if preposterously described (39–46): 44 is less absurd, more genuinely sinister in its inversion to sheer malignity of imagery elsewhere in Crashaw's work always lyrical and positive:

44

The house is hers'd about with a black wood,
Which nods with many a heavy headed tree.
Each flowers a pregnant poyson, try'd and good,
Each herbe a Plague. The winds sighes timed-bee
By a black Fount, which weeps into a flood.
Through the thick shades obscurely might you see
  Minotaures, Cyclopses, with a darke drove
  Of *Dragons, Hydraes, Sphinxes,* fill the Grove.

This concluding couplet begins 18 lines of pagan demi-deities reminiscent of the rout of such at the Christ-Child's birth in Milton's Hymn.

Rest of Book I: Cruelty prepares for her task; arrives at her goal, Herod's palace; tempts the king with dire portents (whispering to him as he sleeps, like the Serpent to Eve in Paradise Lost). *Her aim achieved she hies 'Home to her Hell' leaving him to wake drenched in sweat and fears, vowing to undertake the slaughter, calling up his array to set against the child who 'comes not to rule in wrath, but serve in love', whose soldiers are only a handful of 'rude Shepheards', whose only steeds 'poore Beasts! A slow Oxe, and a simple Asse'. As these phrases show, and others equally could, there are flickers of poetic life within what, in the large, is a dead duck if not quite a turkey.*

Bulla

Quid tibi vana suos offert mea bulla tumores?
  Quid facit ad vestrum pondus inane meum?
Expectat nostros humeros toga fortior; ista
  En mea bulla, lares en tua dextra mihi.

Quid tu? quæ nova machina,
Quæ tam fortuito globo
In vitam properas brevem?
Qualis virgineos adhuc
Cypris concutiens sinus,
Cypris jam nova, jam recens,   10
Et spumis media in suis,
Promsit purpureum latus;
Conchâ de patriâ micas,
Pulchroque exsilis impetu;
Statim & millibus ebria
Ducens terga coloribus
Evolvis tumidos sinus
Sphærâ plena volubili.
Cujus per varium latus,
Cujus per teretem globum   20
Iris lubrica cursitans
Centum per species vagas,
Et picti facies chori
Circum regnat, & undique
Et se Diva volatilis
Jucundo levis impetu
Et vertigine perfidâ
Lascivâ sequitur fugâ
Et pulchrè dubitat; fluit
Tam fallax toties novis,   30
Tot se per reduces vias,
Errorésque reciprocos
Spargit vena Coloribus;
Et pompâ natat ebriâ.
Tali militiâ micans

Bubble

Why does my vain bubble present its orb?
    What does my trifle offer your serious mind?
A more substantial toga awaits my shoulders;
    Here is my *bulla*; you see, your hand is my *lares*.

What weird artifice are you,
Formed as a ball by chance,
In haste to a moment's life?
As Venus, shaking the water
From off still-maidenly breasts –
As Venus, so new, so fresh,
Even yet in the midst of the spray,
Raised up her glistening body;
Even thus, you twinkle forth
From your very own native shell,
And exult with a gorgeous impulse!
At once, you stretch your back,
Drunk with myriad colours;
You spin your plumptious curves
In a full and reeling sphere!
Throughout your varying side,
Throughout your polished globe,
A slippery Iris – coursing
Through a hundred shifting forms
And sheens of dancing dyes –
Rules the round; all over,
The gliding rainbow Goddess,
Giddy with playful assailment
And treacherous gyrations,
Chases herself in lascivious
Flight, and winsomely founders;
And how the beguiler flows!
So many times over and over!
So often down routes retraced,
And mazy wavering ways,
She trails a vein of colours
And swims in a drunken pomp.
With such warfare, the fickle

Agmen se rude dividit;
Campis quippe volantibus,
Et campi levis æquore
Ordo insanus obambulans
Passim se fugit, & fugat; 40
Passim perdit, & invenit.
Pulchrum spargitur hîc Chaos.
Hîc viva, hîc vaga flumina
Ripâ non propriâ meant,
Sed miscent socias vias,
Communique sub alveo
Stipant delicias suas.
Quarum proximitas vaga
Tam discrimine lubrico,
Tam subtilibus arguit 50
Juncturam tenuem notis,
Pompa ut florida nullibi
Sinceras habeat vias;
Nec vultu niteat suo.
Sed dulcis cumulus novos
Miscens purpureos sinus
Flagrat divitiis suis,
Privatum renuens jubar.
Floris diluvio vagi,
Floris Sydere publico 60
Latè ver subit aureum,
Atque effunditur in suæ
Vires undique Copiæ.
Nempe omnis quia cernitur,
Nullus cernitur hîc color,
Et vicinia contumax
Allidit species vagas.
Illîc contiguis aquis
Marcent pallidulæ faces.
Undæ hîc vena tenellulæ, 70
Flammis ebria proximis

Phalanx divides, a-sparkle;
In whirling battlefields –
In the plain of a weightless field –
The crazy, ambling rank
Everywhere flees itself
And puts itself to flight;
Everywhere loses itself,
And everywhere finds itself.
It is beautiful Chaos, displayed!
Here, living, roving rivers
Spill over each other's banks,
And mix their united paths,
And into one common channel
Collate their lovely charms:
Their intimate interfusion,
So slippily distinguished,
Shows them blent so subtly
With their delicate speckles, that nowhere
In all this flowery triumph
Will any convivial runnel
Trace out an ingenuous pathway,
Beam out with its own bright face;
But the sweet superflux,
In which are intermingled
Strange and gleaming verges,
Blazes with its own riches
(Spurning a private splendour); –
A deluge of drifting flowers,
A constellation of flowers
A-glint for all to gaze on!
Golden Spring advances,
Its potency outpouring
In swamping amplitude;
And since you see *all* colours,
You see no colour at all:
So saucy Similitude
Assaults the face of vagueness.
The firebrand limply dwindles
At the inching touch of water;
The streak of a darling wave,
Drunk with the nearing flames,

Discit purpureas vias,
El rubro salit alveo.
Ostri Sanguineum jubar
Lambunt lactea flumina;
Suasu cærulei maris
Mansuescit seges aurea;
Et lucis faciles genæ
Vanas ad nebulas stupent;
Subque uvis rubicundulis   80
Flagrant sobria lilia.
Vicinis adeo rosis
Vicinæ invigilant nives,
Ut sint & niveæ rosæ,
Ut sint & roseæ nives,
Accenduntque rosæ nives,
Extinguuntque nives rosas.
Illîc cum viridi rubet,
Hîc & cum rutilo viret
Lascivi facies chori.   90
Et quicquid rota lubrica
Caudæ stelligeræ notat,
Pulchrum pergit in ambitum.
Hîc cœli implicitus labor,
Orbes orbibus obvii;
Hîc grex velleris aurei
Grex pellucidus ætheris;
Qui noctis nigra pascua
Puris morsibus atterit;
Hîc quicquid nitidum et vagum   100
Cæli vibrat arenula
Dulci pingitur en joco.
Hîc mundus tener impedit
Sese amplexibus in suis.
Succinctique sinu globi
Errat per proprium decus.
Hîc nictant subitæ faces,
Et ludunt tremulum diem.
Mox se surripiunt sui &
Quaerunt tecta supercilî;   110

Is taught a glowing track
And cavorts in its reddening straits.
Milky white rivers lap
The bloody gleam of purple;
The golden corn is tamed
By the blue sea's cajoling;
And the mellow cheeks of daylight
The empty fog confounds.
Sober lilies burn
At the foot of ruddying grapevines;
The neighbouring snows watch over
Even the neighbouring roses;
And a snowy rosebush grows!
And now there are rosy snows!
And the rose lights up the snows,
And the snows snuff out the rose; –
The face of the frolicking chorus
Here wedded to green, is yonder
Garnished with autumn red;
And whatever the sliding wheel
With its starry train discloses,
This ball in its beautiful ambit
Mocks: the tangles of heaven,
With planets intercrossing;
The flock of golden fleeces –
The pellucid flock of the aether,
Which, with cleanly bites,
Nibbles on night's black pasture.
Here, whatever of glitter
And diaphanous disposition
Shakes in heaven's arena,
Lo! here it is painted in jest!
Here, the tender world hampers
Itself in its own embraces,
And in her little, bounded,
Spheral orbit, saunters
Around her own delights;
Sudden torches flare,
And play out their tremulous day:
Anon they steal away
And return to their haughtier homes,

Atque abdunt petulans jubar,
Subsiduntque proterviter.
Atque hæc omnia quam brevis
Sunt mendacia machinæ!
Currunt scilicèt omnia
Sphærâ, non vitreâ quidem,
(Ut quondam siculus globus)
Sed vitro nitidâ magis,
Sed vitro fragili magis,
Et vitro vitreâ magis.   120

   Sum venti ingenium breve
Flos sum, scilicet, aëris,
Sidus scilicet æquoris;
Naturæ jocus aureus,
Naturæ vaga fabula,
Naturæ breve somnium.
Nugarum decus & dolor;
Dilcis, doctaque vanitas.
Auræ filia perfidæ;
Et risus facilis parens.   130
Tantùm gutta superbior,
Fortunatius & lutum.
   Sum fluxæ pretium spei;
Una ex Hesperidum insulis.
Formæ pyxis, amantium
Clarè cæcus ocellulus;
Vanæ & cor leve gloriæ.

   Sum cæcæ speculum Deæ.
Sum fortunæ ego tessera,
Quam dat militibus suis;   140
Sum fortunæ ego symbolum,
Quo sancit fragilem fidem
Cum mortalibus Ebriis
Obsignatque tabellulas.
   Sum blandum, petulans, vagum,
Pulchrum, purpureum, et decens,
Comptum, floridulum, et recens,

46

Veil their freakish dazzle,
And recklessly subside.
And all these things (how brief!)
Are delusions of artifice!
Yea, all of them run their courses
In a sphere not even of glass
(Like the old Sicanian globe);
But more brilliant than glass;
But brittler than glass;
And glassier than glass.

I am the fleeting essence
Of the wind. Yea, I am the blossom
Of air; yea, a star made of water;
Nature's lovely whim,
Nature's nebulous fable,
Nature's passing dream;
The bedecker and sorrow of trifles,
A vanity sweet and clever;
The disloyal breeze's daughter,
And the mother of genial smiles;
A water-drop, only prouder;
No more than mire, – but charmed.
I am the reward
Of transitory hope,
I am one of the isles
Of the Hesperides;
A box for beauty, the clear,
Blind little eye of lovers,
And the gossamer heart of vainglory.
I am the looking-glass
Of the blind goddess, Fortune;
I am Fortune's token
Given to her own soldiers;
I am, even I, her symbol,
The seal that warrants her fragile
Faith with besotted mortals,
And signs her little covenants.
I am blandishing, fickle, vague;
Comely, shining, demure;
Kempt, flowering, fresh;

Distinctum nivibus, rosis,
Undis, ignibus, aëre,
Pictum, gemmeum, & aureum, 150
O sum, (scilicet, O nihil.)

Si piget, et longam traxisse in tædia pompam
  Vivax, & nimiùm Bulla videtur anus;
Tolle tuos oculos, pensum leve defluet, illam
  Parca metet facili non operosa manu.
Vixit adhuc. Cur vixit? adhuc tu nempe legebas;
  Nempe fuit tempus tum potuisse mori.

With spaces of snow and of rose,
And billows, and fires, and air;
Tinted, bejewelled, and lustrous;
I am – O! – nay, o, I am nothing.

If you chide, that my bubble has too much protracted her pomp,
    To the bourn of boredom, and grown too old a dame,
Lift up your eyes, and its flimsy weight will flee;
    Fate's labourless hand can easily cut her off.
She has lived this long; and why? You were reading till now.
    There was plenty of time before now for her to have died.

[A.W.]

II
Sacred, Part 1: *Steps to the Temple*

The Preface to the Reader

Learned Reader,

The Authors friend, will not usurpe much upon thy eye: This is onely for those, whom the name of our Divine Poet hath not yet seized into admiration, I dare undertake, that what Jamblicus (in vita Pythagoræ) *affirmeth of his Master, at his Contemplations, these Poems can, viz. They shal lift thee Reader, some yards above the ground: and, as in* Pythagoras Schoole, *every temper was first tuned into a height by severall proportions of Musick; and spiritualiz'd for one of his weighty Lectures; So maist thou take a Poem hence, and tune thy soule by it, into a heavenly pitch; and thus refined and borne up upon the wings of meditation, in these Poems thou maist talke freely of God, and of that other state.*

Here's Herbert's *second, but equall, who hath retriv'd Poetry of late, and return'd it up to its Primitive use; Let it bound back to heaven gates, whence it came. Thinke yee, St.* Augustine *would have steyned his graver Learning with a booke of Poetry, had he fancied their dearest end to be the vanity of Love-Sonnets, and Epithalamiums? No, no, he thought with this, our Poet, that every foot in a high-borne verse, might helpe to measure the soule into that better world:* Divine Poetry; *I dare hold it, in position against* Suarez *on the subject, to be the Language of the Angels; it is the Quintessence of Phantasie and discourse center'd in Heaven; 'tis the very Outgoings of the soule; 'tis what alone our Author is able to tell you, and that in his owne verse.*

It were prophane but to mention here in the Preface those under-headed Poets, Retainers to seven shares and a halfe; Madrigall fellowes, whose onely businesse in verse, is to rime a poore six-penny soule, a Subburb sinner into hell;—May such arrogant pretenders to Poetry vanish, with their prodigious issue of tumorous heats and flashes of their adulterate braines, and for ever after, may this our Poet fill up the better roome of man. Oh! when the generall arraignment of Poets shall be, to give an accompt of their higher soules, with what a triumphant brow, shall our divine Poet sit above, and looke downe upon poore Homer, Virgil, Horace, Claudian? *&c. who had amongst them the ill lucke to talke out a great part of their gallant Genius, upon Bees, Dung, froggs, and Gnats, &c. and not as himselfe here, upon Scriptures, divine Graces, Martyrs and Angels.*

Reader, we stile his Sacred Poems, Stepps to the Temple, *and aptly, for in the Temple of God, under his wing, he led his life in* St. Maries *Church neere* St. Peters *Colledge: There he lodged under* Tertullian's *roofe of Angels: There he made his nest more gladly then* David's *Swallow neere the house of God: where like a primitive Saint, he offered more prayers in the night, then others usually offer in the day; There, he penned these Poems,* Stepps *for happy soules to climbe heaven by.*

And those other of his pieces intituled, The Delights of the Muses, *(though of a more humane mixture) are as sweet as they are innocent.*

The praises that follow are but few of many that might be conferr'd on him, hee was excellent in five Languages (besides his Mother tongue) vid. Hebrew, Greek, Latine, Italian, Spanish, the two last whereof hee had little helpe in, they were of his owne acquisition.

Amongst his other accomplishments in Accademick (as well pious as harmlesse arts) hee made his skill in Poetry, Musicke, Drawing, Limming, graving, (exercises of his curious invention and sudden fancy) to bee but his subservient recreations for vacant houres, not the grand businesse of his soule.

To the former Qualifications I might adde that which would crowne them all, his rare moderation in diet (almost Lessian temperance) hee never created a Muse out of distempers, nor (with our Canary scribblers) cast any strange mists of surfets before the Intelectuall beames of his mind or memory, the latter of which, hee was so much a master of, that hee had there under locke and key in readinesse, the richest treasures of the best Greeke and Latine Poets, some of which Authors hee had more at his command by heart, then others that onely read their workes, to retaine little, and understand lesse.

Enough Reader, I intend not a volume of praises, larger then his booke, nor need I longer transport thee to thinke over his vast perfections, I will conclude all that I have impartially writ of this Learned young Gent. (now dead to us) as hee himselfe doth, with the last line of his Poem upon Bishop Andrews *Picture before his Sermons*

Verte paginas.

—Look on his following leaves, and see him breath.

The Weeper

1   Haile *Sister Springs,*
              Parents of Silver-forded rills!
                  Ever bubling things!
               Thawing Christall! Snowy Hills!
Still spending, never spent; I meane
Thy faire Eyes sweet *Magdalene.*

2   Heavens thy faire Eyes bee,
              Heavens of ever-falling stars,
                 Tis seed-time still with thee
              And stars thou sow'st whose harvest dares
Promise the earth; to countershine
What ever makes Heavens fore-head fine.

3   But wee are deceived all,
              Stars they are indeed too true,
                 For they but seeme to fall
              As Heavens other spangles doe:
It is not for our Earth and us,
To shine in things so pretious.

4   Upwards thou dost weepe,
              Heavens bosome drinks the gentle streame.
                 Where th' milky rivers meet,
              Thine Crawles above and is the Creame.
Heaven, of such faire floods as this,
Heaven the Christall Ocean is.

5   Every morne from hence,
              A briske Cherub something sips
                 Whose soft influence
              Adds sweetnesse to his sweetest lips.
Then to his Musicke, and his song
Tastes of this breakefast all day long.

6   When some new bright guest
              Takes up among the stars a roome,
                 And Heaven will make a feast,
              Angels with their Bottles come;

And draw from these full Eyes of thine,
Their Masters water, their owne Wine.

7   The dew no more will weepe,
          The Primroses pale cheeke to decke,
          The deaw no more will sleepe,
          Nuzzel'd in the Lillies necke.
Much rather would it tremble heere,
And leave them both to bee thy Teare.

8   Not the soft Gold which
          Steales from the Amber-weeping Tree,
          Makes sorrow halfe so Rich,
          As the drops distil'd from thee.
Sorrowes best Jewels lye in these
Caskets, of which Heaven keeps the Keyes.

9   When sorrow would he seene
          In her brightest Majesty,
          (For shee is a Queen)
          Then is shee drest by none but thee.
Then, and onely then shee weares
Her richest Pearles, I meane thy Teares.

10   Not in the Evenings Eyes
          When they red with weeping are,
          For the Sun that dyes,
          Sits sorrow with a face so faire.
Nowhere but heere did ever meet
Sweetnesse so sad, sadnes so sweet.

11   Sadnesse all the while
          Shee sits in such a Throne as this,
          Can doe nought but smile,
          Nor beleeves shee sadnesse is.
Gladnesse it selfe would bee more glad
To bee made so sweetly sad.

12   There is no need at all
          That the Balsame-sweating bough
          So coyly should let fall,
          His med'cinable Teares; for now
Nature hath learn't t' extract a dew,
More soveraigne and sweet from you.

13   Yet let the poore drops weepe,
          Weeping is the ease of woe,
          Softly let them creepe
          Sad that they are vanquish't so,
They, though to others no releife
May Balsame bee for their own grief.

14   Golden though hee bee,
          Golden *Tagus* murmurs though,
          Might hee flow from thee
          Content and quiet would he goe,
Richer far does he esteeme
Thy silver, then his golden streame.

15   Well does the *May* that lyes
          Smiling in thy cheekes, confesse,
          The *April* in thine eyes,
          Mutuall sweetnesse they expresse.
No *April* e're lent softer showres,
Nor *May* returned fairer flowers.

16   Thus dost thou melt the yeare
          Into a weeping motion,
          Each minute waiteth heere;
          Takes his teare and gets him gone;
By thine eyes tinct enobled thus
Time layes him up: he's pretious.

17   Time as by thee he passes,
          Makes thy ever-watry eyes
          His Hower-Glasses.
          By them his steps he rectifies.
The sands he us'd no longer please,
For his owne sands hee'l use thy seas.

18   Does thy song lull the Ayre?
   Thy teares just Cadence still keeps time.
    Does thy sweet breath'd *Prayer*
   Up in clouds of Incense climbe?
 Still at each sigh, that is each stop:
 A bead, that is a teare doth drop.

19   Does the Night arise?
   Still thy teares doe fall, and fall.
    Does night loose her eyes?
   Still the fountaine weeps for all.
 Let night or day doe what they will
 Thou hast thy taske, thou weepest still.

20   Not, so long she liv'd,
   Will thy tombe report of thee
    But *so long she greiv'd,*
   Thus must we date thy memory.
 Others by Dayes, by Monthes, by Yeares
 Measure their Ages, Thou by Teares.

21   Say watry Brothers
   Yee simpering sons of those faire eyes,
    Your fertile Mothers.
   What hath our world that can entice
 You to be borne? what is't can borrow
 You from her eyes swolne wombes of sorrow.

22   Whither away so fast?
   O whither? for the sluttish Earth
    Your sweetnesse cannot tast
   Nor does the dust deserve your Birth.
 Whither hast ye then? o say
 Why yee trip so fast away?

23   We goe not to seeke
   The darlings of *Aurora's* bed,
    The Roses modest cheeke
   Nor the Violets humble head.
 No such thing; we goe to meet
 A worthier object, *Our Lords* feet.

The Teare

1   What bright soft thing is this?
   Sweet *Mary* thy faire Eyes expence?
    A moist sparke it is,
   A watry Diamond; from whence
The very Terme, I think, was found
The water of a *Diamond*.

2   O 'tis not a Teare,
   'Tis a starre about to drop
    From thine eye its spheare;
   The Sunne will stoope and take it up.
Proud will his sister be to weare
This thine eyes Jewell in her Eare.

3   O 'tis a Teare,
   Too true a Teare; for no sad eyne,
    How sad so e're
   Raine so true a Teare as thine;
Each Drop leaving a place so deare,
Weeps for it selfe, is its owne Teare.

4   Such a Pearle as this is,
   (Slipt from *Aurora's* dewy Brest)
    The Rose buds sweet lip kisses
   And such the Rose its selfe when vext
With ungentle flames, does shed,
Sweating in too warme a Bed.

5   Such the Maiden Gemme
   By the wanton Spring put on,
    Peeps from her Parent stemme,
   And blushes on the manly Sun:
This watry Blossome of thy Eyne
Ripe, will make the richer Wine.

6   Faire Drop, why quak'st thou so?
   'Cause thou streight must lay thy Head

In the Dust? ô no;
The Dust shall never bee thy Bed:
A pillow for thee will I bring,
Stuft with Downe of Angels wing.

7   Thus carryed up on high,
(For to Heaven thou must goe)
Sweetly shalt thou lye,
And in soft slumbers bath thy woe;
Till the singing Orbes awake thee,
And one of their bright Chorus make thee.

8   There thy selfe shalt bee
An eye, but not a weeping one,
Yet I doubt of thee,
Whither th'hadst rather there have shone
An eye of Heaven; or still shine here
In th'Heaven of *Mary's* eye, a *Teare*.

In the Holy Nativity of our Lord God

A Hymn sung as by the Shepheards

CHORUS

Come we shepheards whose blest Sight
  Hath mett love's Noon in Nature's night;
Come lift we up our loftyer Song
  And wake the SUN that lyes too long.

To all our world of well-stoln joy
  He slept; and dream't of no such thing.
While we found out Heavn's fairer ey
  And Kis't the Cradle of our KING.
Tell him He rises now, too late
To show us aught worth looking at.   10

Tell him we now can show Him more
  Then He e're show'd to mortall Sight;
Then he Himselfe e're saw before;
  Which to be seen needes not His light.
Tell him, Tityrus, where th'hast been
Tell him, Thyrsis, what th'hast seen.

Tityrus. Gloomy night embrac't the Place
  Where The Noble Infant lay.
The BABE look't up & shew'd his Face;
  In spite of Darknes, it was DAY.   20
It was THY day, SWEET! & did rise
Not from the EAST, but from thine EYES.

     Chorus   It was THY day, Sweet

Thyrs. WINTER chidde aloud; & sent
  The angry North to wage his warres.
The North forgott his feirce Intent;
  And left perfumes in stead of scarres.
By those sweet eyes' persuasive powrs
Where he mean't frost, he scatter'd flowrs.

Both. We saw thee in thy baulmy Nest,
   Young dawn of our æternall DAY!
We saw thine eyes break from their EASTE
   And chase the trembling shades away.
We saw thee; & we blest the sight
We saw thee by thine own sweet light.

Tity. Poor WORLD (said I.) what wilt thou doe
   To entertain this starry STRANGER?
Is this the best thou canst bestow?
   A cold, and not too cleanly, manger?   40
Contend, ye powres of heav'n & earth.
To fitt a bed for this huge birthe.

      Cho.   Contend ye powers

Thyr. Proud world, said I; cease your contest
   And let the MIGHTY BABE alone.
The Phœnix builds the Phœnix' nest.
   Love's architecture is his own.
The BABE whose birth embraves this morn,
Made his own bed e're he was born.

      Cho.   The BABE whose.

Tit. I saw the curl'd drops, soft & slow,
   Come hovering o're the place's head;
Offring their whitest sheets of snow
   To furnish the fair INFANT's bed
Forbear, said I; be not too bold.
Your fleece is white But t'is too cold.

      Cho.   Forbear, sayd I

Thyr. I saw the obsequious SERAPHIMS
   Their rosy fleece of fire bestow.
For well they now can spare their wings   60
   Since HEAVN itself lyes here below.

62

Well done, said I: but are you sure
Your down so warm, will passe for pure?

      Cho.   Well done sayd I

Tit. No no. your KING'S not yet to seeke
   Where to repose his Royall HEAD
See see, how soon his new-bloom'd CHEEK
   Twixt's mother's brests is gone to bed.
Sweet choise, said we! no way but so
Not to ly cold, yet sleep in snow.   70

      Cho.   Sweet choise, said we.

Both. We saw thee in thy baulmy nest,
   Bright dawn of our æternall Day!
We saw thine eyes break from their EAST
   And chase the trembling shades away.
We saw thee & we blest the sight.
We saw thee, by thine own sweet light.

Cho.   We saw thee, &c.

   FULL CHORUS.

Wellcome, all WONDERS in one sight!
   Æternity shutt in a span.   80
Sommer in Winter. Day in Night.
   Heaven in earth, & GOD in MAN.
Great little one! whose all-embracing birth
Lifts earth to heaven, stoopes heav'n to earth.

WELLCOME. Though nor to gold nor silk.
   To more then Cæsar's birthright is;
Two sister-seas of Virgin-Milk,
   With many a rarely-temper'd kisse
That breathes at once both MAID & MOTHER,
Warmes in the one, cooles in the other.   90

WELLCOME, though not to those gay flyes.
   Guilded ith' Beames of earthly kings;

Slippery soules in smiling eyes
  But to poor Shepheards, home-spun things:
Whose Wealth's their flock; whose witt, to be
  Well read in their simplicity.
Yet when young April's husband showrs
  Shall blesse the fruitfull Maja's bed
We'l bring the First-born of her flowrs
  To kisse thy FEET & crown thy HEAD.   100
To thee, dread lamb! whose love must keep
  The shepheards, more then they the sheep.
To THEE, meek Majesty! soft KING
  Of Simple GRACES & sweet LOVES.
Each of us his lamb will bring
  Each his pair of sylver Doves;
Till burnt at last in fire of Thy fair eyes,
  Our selves become our own best SACRIFICE.

A Hymn to the Name and Honor of the Admirable Sainte Teresa

Foundresse of the Reformation of the Discalced Carmelites, both men & Women; a WOMAN for Angelicall heigth of speculation, for Masculine courage of performance, more then a woman. WHO Yet a Child, out ran maturity, and durst plot a Martyrdome; but was reserved by God to dy the *living death* of the *life* of his *love*. Of whose great impressions as her noble heart had most high experiment, so hath she in her life most heroically exprest them, and in these her heavnly writings most sublimely, most sweetly taught them to ye world.

Love, thou art Absolute sole lord
Of Life & Death. To prove the word,
Wee'l now appeal to none of all
Those thy old Souldiers, Great & tall,
Ripe Men of Martyrdom, that could reach down
With strong armes, their triumphant crown;
Such as could with lusty breath
Speak lowd into the face of death
Their Great Lord's glorious name, to none
Of those whose spatious Bosomes spread a throne   10
For Love at larg to fill: spare blood & sweat;
And see him take a private seat,
Making his mansion in the mild
And milky soul of a soft child.

   Scarse has she learn't to lisp the name
   Of Martyr; yet she thinks it shame
   Life should so long play with that breath
   Which spent can buy so brave a death.

She never undertook to know
What death with love should have to doe;   20
Nor has she e're yet understood
Why to show love, she should shed blood
Yet though she cannot tell you why,
She can Love, & she can Dy.

65

Scarse has she Blood enough to make
A guilty sword blush for her sake;
Yet has she'a HEART dares hope to prove
How much lesse strong is DEATH then LOVE.

Be love but there; let poor six yeares
Be pos'd with the maturest Feares   30
Man trembles at, you straight shall find
LOVE knowes no nonage, nor the MIND.
'Tis LOVE, not YEARES or LIMBS that can
Make the Martyr, or the man.

LOVE touch't her HEART, & lo it beates
High, & burnes with such brave heates;
Such thirsts to dy, as dares drink up,
A thousand cold deaths in one cup.
Good reason. For she breathes All fire.
Her weake brest heaves with strong desire   40
Of what she may with fruitles wishes
Seek for amongst her MOTHER's kisses.

Since 'tis not to be had at home
She'l travail to a Martyrdom.
No home for hers confesses she
But where she may a Martyr be.
   Sh'el to the Moores; And trade with them,
   For this unvalued Diadem.
   She'l offer them her dearest Breath,
   With CHRIST's Name in't, in change for death.   50
   Sh'el bargain with them; & will give
   Them GOD; teach them how to live
   In him: or, if they this deny,
   For him she'l teach them how to Dy.
So shall she leave amongst them sown
Her LORD's Blood; or at least her own.

FAREWEL then, all the world! Adieu.
TERESA is no more for you.
Farewell, all pleasures, sports, & joyes,
(Never till now esteemed toyes)   60
Farewell what ever deare may bee,
MOTHER's armes or FATHER's knee

Farewell house, & farewell home!
SHE'S for the Moores, & MARTYRDOM.

  SWEET, not so fast! lo thy fair Spouse
  Whom thou seekst with so swift vowes,
  Calls thee back, & bidds thee come
  T'embrace a milder MARTYRDOM.

  Blest powres forbid, Thy tender life
Should bleed upon a barborous knife;   70
Or some base hand have power to race
Thy Brest's chast cabinet, & uncase
A soul kept there so sweet, ô no;
Wise heavn will never have it so
THOU art love's victime; & must dy
A death more mysticall & high.
Into love's armes thou shalt let fall
A still-surviving funerall.

His is the DART must make the DEATH
Whose stroke shall tast thy hallow'd breath;   80
A Dart thrice dip't in that rich flame
Which writes thy spouse's radiant Name
Upon the roof of Heav'n; where ay
It shines, & with a soveraign ray
Beates bright upon the burning faces
Of soules which in that name's sweet graces
Find everlasting smiles. So rare,
So spirituall, pure, & fair
Must be th'immortall instrument
Upon whose choice point shall be sent   90
A life so lov'd; And that there be
Fitt executioners for Thee,
The fair'st & first-born sons of fire
Blest SERAPHIM, shall leave their quire
And turn love's souldiers, upon THEE
To exercise their archerie.

  O how oft shalt thou complain
  Of a sweet & subtle PAIN.

Of intolerable JOYES;
Of a DEATH, in which who dyes   100
Loves his death, and dyes again.
And would for ever so be slain.
And lives, & dyes; and knowes not why
To live, But that he thus may never leave to DY.

How kindly will thy gentle HEART
Kisse the sweetly-killing DART!
And close in his embraces keep
Those delicious Wounds, that weep
Balsom to heal themselves with. Thus
When These thy DEATHS, so numerous,   110
Shall all at last dy into one,
And melt thy Soul's sweet mansion;
Like a soft lump of incense, hasted
By too hott a fire, & wasted
Into perfuming clouds, so fast
Shalt thou exhale to Heavn at last
In a resolving SIGH, and then
O what? Ask not the Tongues of men.
Angells cannot tell, suffice,
Thy selfe shall feel thine own full joyes   120
And hold them fast for ever. There
So soon as thou shalt first appear,
The MOON of maiden starrs, thy white
MISTRESSE, attended by such bright
Soules as thy shining self, shall come
And in her first rankes make thee room;
Where 'mongst her snowy family
Immortall wellcomes wait for thee.
  O what delight, when reveal'd LIFE shall stand
And teach thy lipps heav'n with his hand;   130
On which thou now maist to thy wishes
Heap up thy consecrated kisses.
What joyes shall seize thy soul, when she
Bending her blessed eyes on thee
(Those second Smiles of Heav'n) shall dart
Her mild rayes through thy melting heart!

Angels, thy old freinds, there shall greet thee
Glad at their own home now to meet thee.
   All thy good WORKES which went before
And waited for thee, at the door,   140
Shall own thee there; and all in one
Weave a constellation
Of CROWNS, with which the KING thy spouse
Shall build up thy triumphant browes.

All thy old woes shall now smile on thee
And thy paines sitt bright upon thee
All thy sorrows here shall shine,
All thy SUFFRINGS be divine.
TEARES shall take comfort, & turn gemms
And WRONGS repent to Diademms.   150
Ev'n thy DEATHS shall live; & new
Dresse the soul that erst they slew.
Thy wounds shall blush to such bright scarres
As keep account of the LAMB'S warres.

   Those rare WORKES where thou shalt leave writt,
   Love's noble history, with witt
   Taught thee by none but him, while here
   They feed our soules, shall cloth THINE there.
   Each heavnly word by whose hid flame
   Our hard Hearts shall strike fire, the same   160
   Shall flourish on thy browes. & be
   Both fire to us & flame to thee;
   Whose light shall live bright in thy FACE
   By glory, in our hearts by grace.

   Thou shalt look round about, & see
Thousands of crown'd Soules throng to be
Themselves thy crown. Sons of thy vowes
The virgin-births with which thy soveraign spouse
Made fruitfull thy fair soul, goe now
And with them all about thee bow   170
To Him, put on (hee'l say) put on
(My rosy love) That thy rich zone
Sparkling with the sacred flames
Of thousand soules, whose happy names

69

Heav'n keeps upon thy score. (Thy bright
Life brought them first to kisse the light
That kindled them to starrs.) and so
Thou with the LAMB, thy lord, shalt goe;
And whereso'ere he setts his white
Stepps, walk with HIM those wayes of light   180
Which who in death would live to see,
Must learn in life to dy like thee.

from *The Flaming Heart*

Upon the Book and Picture of the seraphicall saint Teresa (as she
is usually expressed with a seraphim biside her)

...

Leave HER alone THE FLAMING HEART.

Leave her that; & thou shalt leave her
Not one loose shaft but love's whole quiver.   70
For in love's feild was never found
A nobler weapon then a WOUND.
Love's passives are his activ'st part.
The wounded is the wounding heart.
O HEART! the æquall poise of lov'es both parts
Bigge alike with wounds & darts.
Live in these conquering leaves; live all the same;
And walk through all tongues one triumphant FLAME
Live here, great HEART; & love and dy & kill;
And bleed & wound; and yeild & conquer still.   80

...

O thou undanted daughter of desires!
By all thy dowr of LIGHTS & FIRES;
By all the eagle in thee, all the dove;
By all thy lives & deaths of love;
By thy larg draughts of intellectuall day,
And by thy thirsts of love more large then they;
By all thy brim-fill'd Bowles of feirce desire
By thy last Morning's draught of liquid fire;   100
By the full kingdome of that finall kisse
That seiz'd thy parting Soul, & seal'd thee his;
By all the heav'ns thou hast in him
(Fair sister of the SERAPHIM!)
By all of HIM we have in THEE;
Leave nothing of my SELF in me.
Let me so read thy life, that I
Unto all life of mine may dy.

In the Glorious ASSUMPTION of Our Blessed Lady
The Hymn

Hark! she is call'd, the parting houre is come.
Take thy Farewell, poor world! heavn must goe home.
A peice of heav'nly earth; Purer & brighter
Then the chast starres, whose choise lamps come to light her
While through the crystall orbes, clearer then they
She climbes; and makes a farre more milkey way.
She's calld. Hark, how the dear immortall dove
Sighes to his sylver mate rise up, my love!
Rise up, my fair, my spottlesse one!
The winter's past, the rain is gone.   10
  The spring is come, the flowrs appear
No sweets, but thou, are wanting here.
       Come away, my love!
       Come away, my dove! cast off delay,
       The court of heav'n is come
       To wait upon thee home; Come come away!
       The flowrs appear.
Or quickly would, wert thou once here.
The spring is come, or if it stay,
'Tis to keep time with thy delay.   20
The rain is gone, except so much as we
Detain in needfull teares to weep the want of thee.
       The winter's past.
       or if he make lesse hast,
His answer is, why she does so.
If sommer come not, how can winter goe.
       Come away, come away.
The shrill winds chide, the waters weep thy stay;
The fountains murmur; & each loftyest tree
Bowes low'st his heavy top, to look for thee.   30
       Come away, my love.
       Come away, my dove &c.
She's call'd again. And will she goe?
When heavn bidds come, who can say no?
Heavn calls her, & she must away.
Heavn will not, & she cannot stay.

GOE then; goe GLORIOUS.
　　　　On the golden wings
Of the bright youth of heavn, that sings
Under so sweet a Burthen. Goe,　　　　　　　　　　　40
Since thy dread son will have it so.
And while thou goest, our song & we
Will, as we may, reach after thee.
HAIL, holy Queen of humble hearts!
We in thy prayse will have our parts.
　　　　Thy pretious name shall be
　　　　Thy self to us; & we
　　　　With holy care will keep it by us.
　　　　We to the last
　　　　Will hold it fast　　　　　　　　　　　　　　50
　　　　And no ASSUMPTION shall deny us.
　　　　All the sweetest showres
　　　　Of our fairest flowres
　　　　Will we strow upon it.
　　　　Though our sweets cannot make
　　　　It sweeter, they can take
　　　　Themselves new sweetnes from it.
MARIA, men & Angels sing
MARIA, mother of our KING.
　LIVE, rosy princesse, LIVE. And may the bright　　　60
Crown of a most incomparable light
Embrace thy radiant browes. O may the best
Of everlasting joyes bath thy white brest.
LIVE, our chast love, the holy mirth
Of heavn; the humble pride of earth.
Live, crown of woemen; Queen of men.
Live mistresse of our song. And when
Our weak desires have done their best,
Sweet Angels come, and sing the rest.

Intermezzo II

A Selection of Sacred Epigrams, in English and Latin

Joann. 5
Ad Bethesdæ piscinam positus.

Quis novus hic refugis incumbit Tantalus undis,
  Quem fallit toties tam fugitiva salus?

Unde hoc naufragium felix? medicæque procellæ?
  Vitáque, tempestas quam pretiosa dedit?

What new Tantalus reclines here on fleeing waters?
  Whom does so fugitive health so often elude?
Whence this fortunate shipwreck? these medicinal storms?
  And Life, which a precious tempest has conferred?

On the water of our Lords Baptism

Each blest drop, on each blest lime
Is washt it selfe, in washing him:
Tis a Gemme while it stayes here,
While it falls hence 'tis a Teare.

Act. 8: On the baptized Æthiopian

Let it not longer be a forlorne hope
                To wash an Æthiope:
He's washt, His gloomy skin a peacefull shade
                For his white soule is made:
And now, I doubt not, the Eternall Dove,
                A black-fac'd house will love.

Joann. 2
Aquæ in vinum versæ.

Unde rubor vestris, & non sua purpura lymphis?
  Quæ rosa mirantes tam nova mutat aquas?

Numen (convivæ) præsens agnoscite Numen:
  Nympha pudica Deum vidit, & erubuit.

Whence to your waves this red, not its native shine?
  What strange new rose transforms the wondering waters?
Acknowledge the Deity, banqueters! He is present:
  The modest Nymph has seen her God, and blushed.

[A.W.]

In (Joh. 17.) Cygnæam D[i] Jesû cantionem.

Quæ mella, ô quot, Christe, favos in carmina fundis!
  Dulcis, & (ah furias!) ah moribundus olor!

Parce tamen; minus hæ si sunt mea gaudia voces:
  Voce quidem dulci, sed moriente canis.

What honey – oh how many honeycombs, Christ,
          you pour into your songs!
  Sweet and – ah madness! – ah, dying swan!
But spare me if these your accents are
          any the less my joys:
  For you sing with a sweet voice, yes! but a dying one.

[A.W.]

and compare:

Ah Hybla's honey, all that sweetness can
Flower in thy song (ô faire, ô dying Swan!)
Yet is the joy I take in't small or none;
It is too sweet to be a long-liv'd one.

[R.C.]

78

Upon the Sepulchre of our Lord.

Here, where our Lord once laid his Head,
Now the Grave lies buried.

The Widowes Mites

Two Mites, two drops, (yet all her house and land)
Falls from a steady Heart, though trembling hand;
The others wanton wealth foams high, and brave,
The other cast away, she onely gave.

Luk. 15.
On the Prodigall.

Tell me bright Boy, tell me my golden Lad,
Whither away so frolick? why so glad?
What all they Wealth in counsaile? all thy state?
Are Husks so deare? troth 'tis a mighty rate.

Matthew 8.
I am not worthy that thou should'st come under my roofe.

Thy God was making hast into thy roofe,
   Thy humble faith and feare keeps him aloofe:
Hee'l be thy Guest, because he may not be,
   Hee'l come – into thy house? no, into thee.

Matth. 27. 12.
Christus accusatus nihil respondit.

Nil ait: *ô sanctæ pretiosa silentia linguæ!*
   Ponderis ô quanti res nihil illud erat!

Ille olim, verbum *qui* dixit, *& omnia* fecit,
   Verbum non dicens *omnia nunc* reficit.

He says *nothing*. Oh precious silence of that sacred tongue!
  Oh how weighty a thing, that no-thing!
He – who once said a word, and made *all* things by it –
  Now, saying *nothing*, remakes them *all* again.

[A.W.]

and compare:

And he answered them nothing.

O Mighty *Nothing*! Unto thee,
Nothing, wee owe all things that bee.
God spake once when hee all things made,
Hee sav'd all when hee *Nothing* said.
The world was made of *Nothing* then;
'Tis made by *Nothyng* now againe.

[R.C.]

On our crucified Lord Naked, and bloody

Th'have left thee naked, Lord, O that they had;
  This Garment too I would they had deny'd.
Thee with thy selfe they have too richly clad,
Opening the purple wardrobe of thy side.
  O never could bee found Garments too good
  For thee to weare, but these, of thine owne blood.

Luc. 18
Pharisæus & Publicanus.

En duo Templum adeunt (diversis mentibus ambo:)
  Ille procul trepido lumine signat humum:

It gravis hic, & in alta ferox penetralia tendit.
  Plus habet hic templi; *plus habet ille* Dei.

Look: two men, of divers minds, approach the Temple.
    One stands afar and eyes the ground with tremulous gaze;
One goes, in solemn zeal, and reaches the innermost chambers.
    He has more of the temple; the other has more of God.

[A.W.]

and compare:

Two went to pray? ô rather say
One went to brag, th'other to pray:

One stands up close and treads on high,
Where th'other dares not send his eye.

One neerer to Gods Altar trod,
The other to the Altars God.

[R.C.]

Joh. 3.
But men loved darknesse rather then Light.

The worlds light shines, shine as it will,
The world will love its Darknesse still;
I doubt though when the World's in Hell,
It will not love its Darknesse halfe so well.

In spinas demtas è Christi capite cruentatas.

Accipe (an ignoscis?) de te sata germina, Miles.
    Quàm segeti est messis discolor illa suæ!

O quæ tam duro gleba est tam grata colono?
    Inserit hic spinas: reddit & illa rosas.

Soldier, take back these shoots – you sowed them, or don't you recall?
    How different a colour comes to the crop of your field!
Oh, to so rough a farmer, what soil would be so benign?
    He plants thorns, and yet it yields him roses.

[A.W.]

and compare:

Upon the Thornes taken downe from our Lords head bloody.

Know'st thou this, Soldier? 'tis a much chang'd plant, which yet
          Thy selfe did'st set,
'Tis chang'd indeed, did Autumn e're such beauties bring
          To shame his Spring?
O! who so hard a husbandman could ever find
          A soyle so kind?
Is not the soile a kind one (thinke ye) that returnes
          Roses for *Thornes*?

[R.C. 1646]

and

UPON THE CROWNE OF THORNS taken downe from the head of our Bl. LORD, all bloody.

Know'st thou This, Soldier? 'Tis a much-chang'd plant which yet
          Thy selfe didst sett.
O who so hard a Husbandman did ever find
          A soile so kind?
Is not the soile a kind one, which returnes
          Roses for Thornes?

[R.C. 1652]

Sacred Fragments

Luke 2. *Quærit Jesum suum Maria.*

And is he gone, whom these armes held but now?
        Their hope, their vow?
Did ever greife, & joy in one poore heart
        Soe soone change part?
Hee's gone. the fair'st flower, that e're bosome drest,
        My soules sweet rest.
My wombes chast pride is gone, my heav'en-borne boy;
        And where is joy?
Hee's gone. & his lov'd steppes to wait upon,
        My joy is gone.   10
My joyes, & hee are gone; my greife, & I
        Alone must ly.
Hee's gone. not leaving with me, till he come,
        One smile at home.
Oh come then, bring thy mother her lost joy:
        Oh come, sweet boy.
Make hast, & come, or e're my greife, & I
        Make hast, & dy.
Peace, heart! the heavens are angry. all their sphæres
        Rivall thy teares.   20
I was mistaken, some faire sphære, or other
        Was thy blest mother.
What, but the fairest heaven, could owne the birth
        Of soe faire earth?
Yet sure thou did'st lodge heere. this wombe of mine
        Was once call'd thine.
Oft have these armes thy cradle envied,
        Beguil'd thy bed.
Oft to thy easy eares hath this shrill tongue
        Trembled, & sung.   30
Oft have I wrapt thy slumbers in soft aires,
        And stroak't thy cares.
Oft hath this hand those silken casements kept,
        While their sunnes slept.
Oft have my hungry kisses made thine eyes
        Too early rise.

Oft have I spoild my kisses daintiest diet,
     To spare thy quiet.
Oft from this breast to thine my love-tost heart
     Hath leapt, to part.   40
Oft my lost soule have I bin glad to seeke
     On thy soft cheeke.
Oft have these armes (alas!) show'd to these eyes
     Their now lost joyes.
Dawne then to me, thou morne of mine owne day,
     And lett heaven stay.
Oh, would'st thou heere still fixe thy faire abode,
     My bosome God:
What hinders, but my bosome still might be
     Thy heaven to thee?   50

from Out of Grotius his Tragedy of Christes Sufferinges

Christ speaks his reproaches: –
Drinke fayling there where I a guest did shine
The Water blush'd, and started into Wine.
Full of high sparkeling vigour: taught by mee
A sweet inebriated extasy.
And streight of all this approbation gate
Good wine in all points. but the easy rate …

from On a prayer booke sent to Mrs. M.R.
     …
Amorous Languishments, Luminous trances,
   Sights which are not seen with eyes,
Spirituall and soule peircing glances.
   Whose pure and subtle lightning, flies
Home to the heart, and setts the house on fire;
And melts it downe in sweet desire
   Yet doth not stay
To aske the windowes leave, to passe that way.   70

Delicious deaths, soft exhalations
Of soule; deare, and divine annihilations.
   A thousand unknowne rites
   Of joyes, and rarifyed delights.

An hundred thousand loves and graces,
   And many a misticke thing,
   Which the divine embraces
Of the deare spowse of spirits with them will bring.
   For which it is no shame,
That dull mortality must not know a name.   80

Of all this hidden store
Of blessings, and ten thousand more;
   If when hee come
Hee find the heart from home,
   Doubtles hee will unload
Himselfe some other where,
   And powre abroad
   His precious sweets,
On the faire soule whom first hee meets.

O faire! ô fortunate! ô rich! ô deare!   90
   O happy and thrice happy shee
   Deare silver breasted dove
     Who ere shee bee,
     Whose early Love
     With winged vowes,
Makes haste to meet her morning spowse:
And close with his immortall kisses.
   Happy soule who never misses,
   To improve that precious houre:
     And every day,   100
     Seize her sweet prey;
   All fresh and fragrant as hee rises,
   Dropping with a balmy showre
   A delicious dew of spices.

O let that happy soule hold fast
Her heavenly armefull, shee shall tast
At once, ten thousand paradises
   Shee shall have power,
   To rifle and deflower,
The rich and roseall spring of those rare sweets,   110
Which with a swelling bosome there shee meets,
Boundlesse and infinite————————

———————————bottomlesse treasures,
            Of pure inebriating pleasures,
Happy soule shee shall discover,
            What joy, what blisse,
            How many heavens at once it is,
To have a God become her lover.

The Recommendation

These Houres, & that which hover's o're my END,
Into thy hands, and hart, lord, I commend.

Take Both to Thine Account, that I & mine
In that Hour, & in these, may be all thine.

That as I dedicate my devoutest BREATH
To make a kind of LIFE for my lord's DEATH,

So from his living, & life-giving DEATH,
My dying LIFE may draw a new, & never fleeting BREATH.

Abraham Cowley's Hope, *intertwined with*
M. Crashaws ANSWER FOR HOPE

Hope whose weak beeing ruin'd is
Alike if it succeed or if it misse!
Whom ill or good does equally confound
And both the homes of fate's dilemma wound.
    Vain shadow; that dost vanish quite
    Both at full noon & perfect night!
The starres have not a possibility
    Of blessing Thee.
If thinges then from their end we happy call,
'Tis hope is the most hopelesse thing of all.   10

    Dear hope! earth's dowry, & heavn's debt!
    The entity of those that are not yet.
    Subtlest, but surest beeing! Thou by whom
    Our nothing has a definition!
        Substantiall shade! whose sweet allay
        Blends both the noones of night & day.
    Fates cannot find out a capacity
        Of hurting thee.
    From Thee their lean dilemma, with blunt horn,
    Shrinkes, as the sick moon from the wholsome morn.

 Hope, thou bold Taster of delight!
Who instead of doing so, devourst it quite.
Thou bringst us an estate, yet leav'st us poor
By clogging it with legacyes before.
    The joyes which we intire should wed
    Come deflour'd-virgins to our bed.
Good fortunes without gain imported be
    Such mighty custom's paid to Thee.
For joy like wine kep't close, does better tast;
If it take air before his spirits wast.

Rich hope! love's legacy, under lock
Of faith! still spending, & still growing stock!
Our crown-land lyes above yet each meal brings
A seemly portion for the sonnes of kings.
            Nor will the virgin joyes we wed
            Come lesse unbroken to our bed,
Because that from the bridall cheek of blisse
            Thou steal'st us down a distant kisse.
Hope's chast stealth harmes no more joye's maidenhead
Then spousall rites prejudge the marriage bed.

Hope, fortun's cheating lottery
Where for one prize, an hundred blankes there be.
Fond archer, hope. Who tak'st thine aime so farr
That still or short or wide thine arrowes are
            Thinne empty cloud which th'ey deceives
            With shapes that our own fancy gives.
A cloud which gilt & painted now appeares
            But must drop presently in teares
When thy false beames o're reason's light prevail,
By IGNES FATUI for north starres we sail.

Fair hope! our earlyer heav'n by thee
Young time is taster to eternity
Thy generous wine with age growes strong, not sowre.
Nor does it kill thy fruit, to smell thy flowre.
            Thy golden, growing, head never hangs down
            Till in the lappe of loves full noone
It falls; and dyes! o no, it melts away
            As does the dawn into the day.
As lumpes of sugar loose themselves; and twine
Their supple essence with the soul of wine.

Brother of fear more gayly clad.
The merryer fool oth two, yet quite as mad.
Sire of repentance, child of fond desire
That blow'st the chymick & the lover's fire.
            Still leading them insensibly'on
            With the strong witchcraft of Anon.
By thee the one does changing nature through
            Her endlesse labyrinth's pursue,

And th'other chases woman; while she goes
More wayes & turnes then hunted nature knowes.

Fortune? alas, above the world's low warres
Hope walks; & kickes the curld heads of conspiring starres.
Her keel cutts not the waves where These winds stirr
Fortune's whole lottery is one blank to her.
Her shafts, and shee fly farre above,
And forrage in the fields of light and love.
Sweet hope! kind cheat! fair fallacy by thee
We are not WHERE nor What we be,
But WHAT & WHERE we would be. Thus art thou
Our absent PRESENCE, and our future Now.
Faith's sister ! nurse of fair desire!
Fear's antidote ! a wise & well-stay'd fire!
Temper twixt chill despair, & torrid joy!
Queen Regent in yonge love's minority!
Though the vext chymick vainly chases
His fugitive gold through all her faces;
Though love's more feirce, more fruitlesse, fires assay
One face more fugitive then all they;
True hope's a glorious hunter & her chase,
The GOD of nature in the feilds of grace.

For Hope
(Abraham Cowley)

1.
Hope, of all Ills that men endure,
The only cheap and *Universal Cure*!
Thou *Captives freedom*, and Thou *sick Mans Health*!
Thou *Losers Victo'ry*, and thou *Beggars wealth*!
Thou *Manna*, which from Heav'n we eat,
To every *Tast* a several *Meat*!
Thou strong *Retreat*! thou sure *entail'd Estate*,
Which nought has power to *alienate*!
Thou pleasant, *honest Flatterer*! for none
Flatter unhappy Men, but thou alone!

2.

Hope, thou *First-fruits* of *Happiness*!
Thou gentle *Dawning* of a bright *Success*!
Thou good *Prepar'ative*, without which our Joy
Does *work* too strong, and whilst it cures, destroy;
    Who out of *Fortunes* reach dost stand,
    And art a blessing *still in hand!*
Whilst *Thee*, her *Earnest-Money* we retain,
    We certain are to gain,
Whether she'her *bargain* break, or else fulfill;
Thou only *good*, not worse, for *ending* ill!

3.

Brother of *Faith*, 'twixt whom and Thee
The joys of *Heav'en* and *Earth* divided be!
Though *Faith* be *Heir*, and have the *fixt estate*,
Thy *Portion* yet in *Moveables* is great.
    Happiness it self's all one
    In *Thee*, or in *possession!*
Only the *Future's Thine*, the *present His!*
    Thine's the more hard and noble bliss;
Best *apprehender* of our joys, which hast
So long a *reach*, and yet canst hold so *fast!*

4.

Hope, thou sad *Lovers* only *Friend!*
Thou *Way* that mayst dispute it with the *End!*
For *Love* I fear's a fruit that does delight
The *Tast* it self less than the *Smell* and *Sight*.
    Fruition more deceitful is
    Than *Thou* canst be, when thou dost *miss*;
Men leave thee by *obtaining*, and strait flee
    Some other way again to *Thee*;
And that's a pleasant *Country*, without doubt,
To which all soon return that travel out.

III
Sacred, Part 2: *Carmen Deo Nostro*

To the Name above Every Name, the Name of Jesus
A Hymn

I Sing the NAME which None can say
But touch't with An interiour RAY:
The Name of our New PEACE; our Good:
Our Blisse: & Supernaturall Blood:
The Name of All our Lives & Loves.
Hearken, And Help, ye holy Doves!
The high-born Brood of Day; you bright
Candidates of blissefull Light,
The HEIRS Elect of Love; whose Names belong
Unto The everlasting life of Song;   10
All ye wise SOULES, who in the wealthy Brest
Of This unbounded NAME build your warm Nest.
Awake, MY glory. SOUL, (if such thou be,
And That fair WORD at all referr to Thee)
   Awake & sing
   And be All Wing;
Bring hither thy whole SELF; & let me see
What of thy Parent HEAVN yet speakes in thee.
   O thou art Poore
   Of noble POWERS, I see,   20
And full of nothing else but empty ME,
Narrow, & low, & infinitely lesse
Then this GREAT mornings mighty Busynes.
   One little WORLD or two
   (Alas) will never doe.
   We must have store.
Goe, SOUL, out of thy Self, & seek for More.
   Goe & request
Great NATURE for the KEY of her huge Chest
Of Heavns, the self involving Sett of Sphears   30
(Which dull mortality more Feeles then heares)
   Then rouse the nest
Of nimble ART, & traverse round
The Aiery Shop of soul-appeasing Sound:
And beat a summons in the Same
   All-soveraign Name
To warn each severall kind

And shape of sweetnes, Be they such
        As sigh with supple wind
        Or answer Artfull Touch,   40
That they convene & come away
To wait at the love-crowned Doores of
        This Illustrious DAY.
Shall we dare This, my Soul? we'l doe't and bring
No Other note for't, but the Name we sing
        Wake LUTE & HARP
        And every sweet-lipp't Thing
        That talkes with tunefull string;
Start into life, And leap with me
Into a hasty Fitt-tun'd Harmony.
        Nor must you think it much   50
        T'obey my bolder touch;
I have Authority in LOVE'S name to take you
And to the worke of Love this morning wake you
        Wake; In the Name
Of HIM who never sleeps, All Things that Are,
        Or, what's the same,
        Are Musicall;
        Answer my Call
        And come along;   60
Help me to meditate mine Immortall Song.
Come, ye soft ministers of sweet sad mirth,
Bring All your houshold stuffe of Heavn on earth;
O you, my Soul's most certain Wings,
Complaining Pipes, & prattling Strings,
        Bring All the store
Of SWEETS you have; And murmur that you have no more.
        Come, nere to part,
        NATURE & ART!
        Come; & come strong,   70
To the conspiracy of our Spatious song.
        Bring All the Powres of Praise
Your Provinces of well-united WORLDS can raise;
Bring All your LUTES & HARPS of HEAVN & EARTH;
What e're cooperates to The common mirthe
        Vessells of Vocall Joyes,
Or You, more noble Architects of Intellectuall Noise,
Cymballs of Heav'n, or Humane sphears,
Solliciters of SOULES or EARES;

And when you'are come, with All   80
That you can bring or we can call;
    O may you fix
    For ever here, & mix
    Your selves into the long
And everlasting series of a deathlesse SONG
Mix All your many WORLDS, Above,
And loose them into ONE of Love.
    Chear thee my HEART!
    For Thou too hast thy Part
    And Place in the Great Throng   90
Of This Unbounded All-imbracing SONG.
    Powres of my Soul, be Proud!
    And speake lowd
To All the dear-bought Nations This Redeeming Name,
And in the wealth of one Rich WORD proclaim
New Similes to Nature.
    May it be no wrong
Blest Heavns, to you, & your Superiour song,
That we, dark Sons of Dust & Sorrow,
    A while Dare borrow   100
The Name of Your Delights & our Desires,
And fitt it to so farr inferior LYRES.
Our Murmurs have their Musick too,
Ye mighty ORBES, as well as you,
    Nor yeilds the noblest Nest
Of warbling SERAPHIM to the eares of Love,
A choicer Lesson then the joyfull BREST
    Of a poor panting Turtle-Dove.
And we, low Wormes have leave to doe
The Same bright Busynes (ye Third HEAVENS) with you.   110
Gentle SPIRITS, doe not complain.
    We will have care
    To keep it fair,
And send it back to you again.
Come, lovely NAME! Appeare from forth the Bright
    Regions of peacefull Light
Look from thine own Illustrious Home,
Fair KING of NAMES, & come.
Leaue All thy native Glories in their Gorgeous Nest,
And give thy Self a while The gracious Guest   120

95

Of humble Soules, that seek to find
   The hidden Sweets
   Which man's heart meets
When Thou art Master of the Mind.
Come, lovely Name; life of our hope!
Lo we hold our HEARTS wide ope!
Unlock thy Cabinet of DAY
Dearest Sweet, & come away.
   Lo how the thirsty Lands
Gasp for thy Golden Showres! with long stretch't Hands 130
   Lo how the laboring EARTH
   That hopes to be
   All Heaven by THEE,
   Leapes at thy Birth.
The'attending WORLD, to wait thy Rise,
   First turn'd to eyes;
And then, not knowing what to doe;
Turn'd Them to TEARES, & spent Them too.
Come ROYALL Name, & pay the expence
Of All this Pretious Patience. 140
   O come away
And kill the DEATH of This Delay.
O see, so many WORLDS of barren yeares
Melted & measur'd out in Seas of TEARES.
O see, The WEARY liddes of wakefull Hope
(LOVE's Eastern windowes) All wide ope
   With Curtains drawn,
To catch The Day-break of Thy DAWN.
O dawn, at last, long look't for Day!
Take thine own wings, & come away. 150
Lo, where Aloft it comes! It comes, Among
The Conduct of Adoring SPIRITS, that throng
Like diligent Bees, And swarm about it.
   O they are wise;
And know what SWEETES are suck't from out it.
   It is the Hive,
   By which they thrive,
Where All their Hoard of Hony lyes.
Lo where it comes, upon The snowy DOVE's
Soft Back; And brings a Bosom big with Loves. 160

WELCOME to our dark world, Thou
                    Womb of Day!
Unfold thy fair Conceptions; And display
The Birth of our Bright Joyes.
                    O thou compacted
Body of Blessings: spirit of Soules extracted!
O dissipate thy spicy Powres
(Clowd of condensed sweets) & break upon us
                    In balmy showrs;
  O fill our senses, And take from us   170
All force of so Prophane a Fallacy
To think ought sweet but that which smells of Thee.
Fair, flowry Name; In none but Thee
And Thy Nectareall Fragrancy,
                    Hourly there meetes
An universall SYNOD of All sweets;
By whom it is defined Thus
                    That no Perfume
                    For ever shall presume
To passe for Odoriferous,   180
But such alone whose sacred Pedigree
Can prove it Self some kin (sweet name) to Thee.
SWEET NAME, in Thy each Syllable
A Thousand Blest ARABIAS dwell;
A Thousand Hills of Frankincense;
Mountains of myrrh, & Beds of spices,
And ten Thousand PARADISES
The soul that tasts thee takes from thence.
How many unknown WORLDS there are
Of Comforts, which Thou hast in keeping!   190
How many Thousand Mercyes there
In Pitty's soft lap ly a sleeping!
Happy he who has the art
                    To awake them,
                    And to take them
Home, & lodge them in his HEART.
O that it were as it was wont to be!
When thy old Freinds of Fire, All full of Thee,
Fought against Frowns with smiles; gave Glorious chase
To Persecutions; And against the Face   200
Of DEATH & feircest Dangers, durst with Brave
And sober pace march on to meet A GRAVE.

On their Bold BRESTS about the world they bore thee
And to the Teeth of Hell stood up to teach thee,
In Center of their inmost Soules they wore thee,
Where Rackes & Torments striv'd, in vain, to reach thee.
   Little, alas, thought They
Who tore the Fair Brests of thy Freinds,
   Their Fury but made way
For Thee; And serv'd therein Thy glorious ends.   210
What did Their weapons but with wider pores
Inlarge thy flaming-brested Lovers
   More freely to transpire
   That impatient Fire
The Heart that hides Thee hardly covers.
What did their Weapons but sett wide the Doores
For Thee: Fair, purple Doores, of love's devising;
The Ruby windowes which inrich't the EAST
Of Thy so oft repeated Rising.
Each wound of Theirs was Thy new Morning;   220
And reinthron'd thee in thy Rosy Nest,
With blush of thine own Blood thy day adorning.
It was the witt of love o'reflowd the Bounds
Of WRATH, & made thee way through All Those WOUNDS.
Wellcome dear, All-Adored Name!
   For sure there is no Knee
   That knowes not THEE.
Or if there be such sonns of shame,
   Alas what will they doe
   When stubborn Rocks shall bow   230
And Hills hang down their Heavn-saluting Heads
   To seek for humble Beds
Of Dust, where in the Bashfull shades of night
Next to their own low NOTHING they may ly,
And couch before the dazeling light of thy dread majesty.
They that by Love's mild Dictate now
   Will not adore thee,
Shall Then with Just Confusion, bow
   And break before thee.

from *Charitas Nimia, or The Dear Bargain*

Lord, what is man? why should he coste thee
So dear? what had his ruin lost thee?
Lord what is man? that thou hast overbought
        So much a thing of nought?

         …

  Alas, sweet lord, what wer't to thee
If there were no such wormes as we?   10
Heav'n ne're the lesse still heavn would be,
        Should Mankind dwell
        In the deep hell.
What have his woes to doe with thee?

        Let him goe weep
        O're his own wounds;
        SERAPHIMS will not sleep
Nor spheares let fall their faithfull rounds.

  Still would The youthfull SPIRITS sing;
And still thy spatious Palace ring.   20
Still would those beauteous ministers of light
        Burn all as bright,

  And bow their flaming heads before thee
Still thrones & Dominations would adore thee
Still would those ever-wakefull sons of fire
        Keep warm thy prayse
        Both nights & dayes,
And teach thy lov'd name to their noble lyre.

         …

        Will the gallant sun
        E're the lesse glorious run?   40
Will he hang down his golden head
Or e're the sooner seek his western bed,
        Because some foolish fly
        Growes wanton, & will dy?

If I were lost in misery,
What was it to thy heavn & thee?
What was it to thy pretious blood
If my foul Heart call'd for a floud?

What if my faithlesse soul & I
      Would needs fall in   50
      With guilt & sin,
What did the Lamb, that he should dy?
What did the lamb, that he should need,
When the wolf sins, himself to bleed?

      If my base lust,
Bargain'd with Death & well-beseeming dust
      Why should the white
      Lamb's bosom write
      The purple name
      Of my sin's shame?   60

Why should his unstaind brest make good
My blushes with his own heart-blood?

O My SAVIOUR, make me see
How dearly thou hast payd for me

That lost again my LIFE may prove
As then in DEATH, so now in love.

Adoro Te
(after S. Thomas Aquinas)

With all the powres my poor Heart hath
Of humble love & loyall Faith,
Thus lowe (my hidden life!) I bow to thee
Whom too much love hath bow'd more low for me.
Down down, proud sense! Discourses dy.
Keep close, my soul's inquiring ey!
Nor touch nor tast must look for more
But each sitt still in his own Dore.

  Your ports are all superfluous here,
Save That which lets in faith, the eare.   10
Faith is my skill. Faith can beleive
As fast as love new lawes can give.
Faith is my force. Faith strength affords
To keep pace with those powrfull words.
And words more sure, more sweet, then they
Love could not think, truth could not say.

  O let thy wretch find that releife
Thou didst afford the faithfull theife.
Plead for me, love! Alleage & show
That faith has farther, here, to goe   20
And lesse to lean on. Because than
Though hidd as GOD, wounds writt thee man,
Thomas might touch; None but might see
At least the suffring side of thee;
And that too was thy self which thee did cover,
But here ev'n That's hid too which hides the other.

  Sweet, consider then, that I
Though allow'd nor hand nor eye
To reach at thy lov'd Face; nor can
Tast thee GOD, or touch thee MAN   30
Both yet beleive; and wittnesse thee
My LORD too & my GOD, as lowd as He.

  Help lord, my Faith, my Hope increase;
And fill my portion in thy peace.

101

Give love for life; nor let my dayes
Grow, but in new powres to thy name & praise.

O dear memoriall of that Death
Which lives still, & allowes us breath!
Rich, Royall food! Bountyfull BREAD!
Whose use denyes us to the dead;   40
Whose vitall gust alone can give
The same leave both to eat & live;
Live ever Bread of loves, & be
My life, my soul, my surer selfe to mee.

O soft self-wounding Pelican!
Whose brest weepes Balm for wounded man.
Ah this way bend thy benign floud
To'a bleeding Heart that gaspes for blood.
That blood, whose least drops soveraign be
To wash my worlds of sins from me.   50
Come love! Come LORD! & that long day
For which I languish, come away.
When this dry soul those eyes shall see,
And think the unseal'd sourse of thee.
When Glory's sun faith's shades shall chase,
And for thy veil give me thy FACE.

AMEN

To the Same Party* Councel concerning her Choise

Dear, heavn-designed SOUL!
Amongst the rest
Of suters that beseige your Maiden brest,
  Why may not I
  My fortune try
And venture to speak one good word
Not for my self alas, but for my dearer LORD?
You'ave seen allready, in this lower sphear
Of froth & bubbles, what to look for here.
Say, gentle soul, what can you find   10
   But painted shapes,
   Peacocks & Apes,
   Illustrious flyes,
Guilded dunghills, glorious LYES,
   Goodly surmises
   And deep disguises,
Oathes of water, words of wind?
TRUTH biddes me say, 'tis time you cease to trust
Your soul to any son of dust.
'Tis time you listen to a braver love,   20
   Which from above
   Calls you up higher
   And biddes you come
   And choose your roome
Among his own fair sonnes of fire,
   Where you among
   The golden throng
That watches at his palace doores
   May passe along
And follow those fair starres of yours;   30
Starrs much too fair & pure to wait upon
The false smiles of a sublunary sun.
Sweet, let me prophesy that at last t'will prove
   Your wary love
Layes up his purer & more pretious vowes,
And meanes them for a farre more worthy SPOUSE
Then this world of Lyes can give ye

*   see p. 28

'Evn for Him with whom nor cost,
Nor love, nor labour can be lost;
Him who never will deceive ye.   40
Let not my lord, the Mighty lover
Of soules, disdain that I discover
           The hidden art
Of his high stratagem to win your heart,
           It was his heavnly art
           Kindly to crosse you
           In your mistaken love,
           That, at the next remove
           Thence he might tosse you
           And strike your troubled heart   50
Home to himself; to hide it in his brest
           The bright ambrosiall nest,
Of love, of life, & everlasting rest.
           Happy Mystake!
           That thus shall wake
Your wise soul, never to be wonne
Now with a love below the sun.
Your first choyce failes, ô when you choose agen
May it not be amongst the sonnes of Men.

A Song

Lord, when the sense of thy sweet grace
Sends up my soul to seek thy face.
Thy blessed eyes breed such desire,
I dy in love's delicious Fire.
  O love, I am thy SACRIFICE.
Be still triumphant, blessed eyes.
Still shine on me, fair suns! that I
Still may behold, though still I dy.

Second part

  Though still I dy, I live again;
Still longing so to be still slain,   10
So gainfull is such losse of breath,
I dy even in desire of death.
  Still live in me this loving strife
Of living DEATH & dying LIFE.
For while thou sweetly slayest me
Dead to my selfe, I live in Thee.

from *A Description of a Religious House and Condition of Life*
(out of Barclay)

No roofes of gold o're riotous tables shining
Whole dayes & suns devour'd with endlesse dining;
No sailes of tyrian sylk proud pavements sweeping;
Nor ivory couches costlyer slumbers keiping;
False lights of flairing gemmes; tumultuous joyes;
Halls full of flattering men & frisking boyes;
Whate're false showes of short & slippery good
Mix the mad sons of men in mutuall blood.
But WALKES & unshorn woods; and soules, just so
Unforc't & genuine; but not shady tho.   10
Our lodgings hard & homely as our fare.
That chast & cheap, as the few clothes we weare.
Those, course & negligent, As the naturall lockes
Of these loose groves, rough as th'unpolish't rockes.
A hasty Portion of præscribed sleep;
Obedient slumbers? that can wake & weep,
And sing, & sigh, & work, and sleep again;
Still rowling a round sphear of still-returning pain.
Hands full of harty labours; Paines that pay
And prize themselves; doe much, that more they may,   20
And work for work, not wages; let to morrow's
New drops, wash off the sweat of this daye's sorrows.
A long & dayly-dying life, which breaths
A respiration of reviving deaths.

    ...

[And] reverent discipline, & religious fear,   30
And soft obedience, find sweet biding here;
Silence, & sacred rest; peace, & pure joyes;
Kind loves keep house, ly close, and make no noise,
And room enough for Monarchs, while none swells
Beyond the kingdomes of contentfull Cells.
The self-remembring SOUL sweetly recovers
Her kindred with the starrs; not basely hovers
Below: But meditates her immortall way
Home to the originall sourse of LIGHT & intellectuall Day.

A Letter from Mr CRASHAW to the Countess of Denbigh, Against Irresolution and Delay in Matters of Religion

What Heav'n-besieged Heart is this
Stands Trembling at the Gate of Blisse:
Holds fast the Door, yet dares not venture
Fairly to open and to enter?
Whose Definition is, A Doubt
'Twixt Life and Death, 'twixt In and Out.
Ah! linger not, lov'd Soul: A slow
And late Consent was a long No.
Who grants at last, a great while try'de,
And did his best to have Deny'de.   10
   What Magick-Bolts, what mystick Barrs
Maintain the Will in these strange Warrs?
What Fatall, yet fantastick, Bands
Keep the free Heart from his own Hands?
Say, lingring Fair, why comes the Birth
Of your brave Soul so slowly forth?
Plead your Pretences, (O you strong
In weaknesse) why you chuse so long
In Labour of your self to ly,
Not daring quite to Live nor Die.   20
   So when the Year takes cold we see
Poor Waters their own Prisoners be
Fetter'd and lock'd up fast they lie
In a cold self-captivity.
Th'astonish'd Nymphs their Floud's strange Fate deplore,
To find themselves their own severer Shoar.
   Love, that lends haste to heaviest things,
In you alone hath lost his wings.
Look round and reade the World's wide face,
The field of Nature or of Grace;   30
Where can you fix, to find Excuse
Or Pattern for the Pace you use?
Mark with what Faith Fruits answer Flowers,
And know the Call of Heav'n's kind showers:
Each mindfull Plant hasts to make good
The hope and promise of his Bud.

Seed-time's not all; there should be Harvest too.
Alas! and has the Year no Spring for you?
    Both Winds and Waters urge their way,
And murmure if they meet a stay.   40
Mark how the curl'd Waves work and wind,
All hating to be left behind.
Each bigge with businesse thrusts the other,
And seems to say, Make haste, my Brother.
The aiery nation of neat Doves,
That draw the Chariot of chast Loves,
Chide your delay: yea those dull things,
Whose wayes have least to doe with wings,
Make wings at least of their own Weight,
And by their Love controll their Fate.   50
So lumpish Steel, untaught to move,
Learn'd first his Lightnesse by his Love.
    What e're Love's matter be, he moves
By th'even wings of his own Doves,
Lives by his own Laws, and does hold
In grossest Metalls his own Gold.
    All things swear friends to Fair and Good,
Yea Suitours; Man alone is wo'ed,
Tediously wo'ed, and hardly wone:
Only not slow to be undone.
As if the Bargain had been driven   60
So hardly betwixt Earth and Heaven;
Our God would thrive too fast, and be
Too much a gainer by't, should we
Our purchas'd selves too soon bestow
On him, who has not lov'd us so.
When love of Us call'd Him to see
If wee'd vouchsafe his company,
He left his Father's Court, and came
Lightly as a Lambent Flame,   70
Leaping upon the Hills, to be
The Humble King of You and Me.
Nor can the cares of his whole Crown
(When one poor Sigh sends for him down)
Detain him, but he leaves behind
The late wings of the lazy Wind,

Spurns the tame Laws of Time and Place,
And breaks through all ten Heav'ns to our embrace.
 Yield to his Siege, wise Soul, and see
 Your Triumph in his Victory.   80
 Disband dull Feares, give Faith the day:
 To save your Life, kill your Delay.
 'Tis Cowardise that keeps this Field;
 And want of Courage not to Yield.
 Yield then, O yield, that Love may win
 The Fort at last, and let Life in.
 Yield quickly, lest perhaps you prove
 Death's Prey, before the Prize of Love.
This Fort of your Fair Self if't be not wone,
He is repuls'd indeed, but You'r undone.   90